1997

To La...

Wit...

wishes.

Reva

Lincoln's
Devotional

Lincoln's Devotional

Introduction by
Carl Sandburg

HENRY HOLT AND COMPANY
NEW YORK

Henry Holt and Company, Inc.
Publishers since 1866
115 West 18th Street
New York, New York 10011

Henry Holt® is a registered
trademark of Henry Holt and Company, Inc.

Published in Canada by Fitzhenry & Whiteside Ltd.,
195 Allstate Parkway, Markham, Ontario L3R 4T8.

Library of Congress Cataloging-in-Publication Data
Believer's daily treasure.
Lincoln's devotional.—1st ed.
p.   cm.
Originally published: London: The believer's daily treasure, or,
Text of scripture arranged for every day in the year. 4th ed. London:
Religious Tract Society, 1852.
1. Devotional calendars.   2. Bible—Devotional literature.
3. Lincoln, Abraham, 1809–1865—Religion.   I. Title.
BV4810.B335   1995
242'.2—dc20   94-39875
                                                                      CIP

ISBN 0-8050-3852-3

Henry Holt books are available for special promotions
and premiums. For details contact: Director, Special Markets.

First Henry Holt Edition—1995

DESIGNED BY BRIAN MULLIGAN

Printed in the United States of America
All first editions are printed on acid-free paper. ∞

1   3   5   7   9   10   8   6   4   2

Introduction

IN DECEMBER of the year 1849, Edward Baker Lincoln, the second of the Lincoln boys, was struck down with illness. It may have been diphtheria. No records of the exact nature of the sickness exist. After fifty-two days of waiting and fear, on the first day of February, Abraham Lincoln held in his arms the white still body of a child of his own. He could call the name of Eddie to his boy, and the boy had no ears to hear nor breath to answer.

This was his own kith and kin, who had come out of silence and gone back to silence, back where Nancy Hanks had gone the year he helped his father peg together a plank coffin. He tried to pierce through into regions of that silence, and find replies to questions that surged in him.

On the day that Eddie was buried, a funeral sermon was pronounced by the Reverend James Smith of the

First Presbyterian Church of Springfield, Illinois, and a friendship developed between the Lincoln family and Mr. Smith. The minister had been a wild boy in his young days in Scotland, had been a scoffer at religion, and then had become a preacher in Kentucky. He could tell a story—he and Lincoln were good company. "A good story," said Lincoln, "is medicine to my bones."

It wasn't long after Eddie's death that the Lincolns rented a pew in the church. In 1852 Mrs. Lincoln took the sacrament and joined in membership. Pastor Smith presented Lincoln with a copy of his book, "The Christian's Defense," a reply to infidels and atheists. Lincoln read the book, said he was interested, later attended revival meetings held in the church, and served in several capacities, but when asked to join the church, said he "couldn't quite see it."

In the same year, the Religious Tract Society of London, England, published a daily devotional titled "The Believer's Daily Treasure; or, Texts of Scripture Arranged for Every Day in the Year." On the title page appeared this verse from Psalm CXIX:72:

The law of thy mouth is better unto
me than thousands of gold and silver

How Abraham Lincoln acquired his copy of the devotional we do not know. In 1852 he received as a gift at least one other book concerned with religion, but there is no word to be found of "The Believer's Daily Treasure." It could have been a gift from Mary Lincoln; sometime after 1847, Lincoln gave her a large family Bible, and perhaps this handy, vest-pocket book was a present from her in return, one he could carry with him for occasional reading on the Old Eighth Circuit. We do know that on the inside cover of the tiny book of Scripture and verse, Lincoln signed his name with typical abbreviation. And from this we can surmise that either the volume itself or the person who presented it to him was held in deep regard, for throughout his life Lincoln was sparing in the number of books in which he wrote his name. His signature, it would seem, was inscribed more as an expression of strong interest or affection than as a precaution against a book's becoming lost, strayed, stolen.

From his earliest reading days as a boy, Lincoln turned the pages of the Bible, and over all the years of his life he went on with his reading of it, often quoting from it in private conversations and public addresses. He and his family owned several Bibles. Writing to Mary, the sister of his best friend, Joshua Speed, he said, "Tell your mother that I have not got her present with me, but I intend to read it regularly when I return home." The gift was an Oxford Bible. In 1864 he received a beautiful Bible from a group of Negroes from Baltimore. In acknowledging the gift, Lincoln said, "In regard to this great book, I have but to say it is the best gift God has given to man."

Among universal possessions of the American people are certain speeches and letters of Lincoln that are colored and in part drenched with biblical references and learning. Why did Lincoln say "Four score and seven" instead of the plain figure "eighty-seven" at the opening of his Gettysburg speech? Probably, it has been suggested, because in the Old Testament it reads most often "two score" instead of "forty," and "four score" instead of "eighty." In the Second Inaugural he spoke as an interpreter of the purposes of the Almighty, as a familiar of the pages of Holy Writ: "The Almighty has his own purposes. 'Woe unto the world because of offences: For it must needs be that offences come; but woe to that man by whom the offence cometh.' "

In this Second Inaugural address, of biblical derivation is the expression, "Let us judge not, that we be not judged." As the end of the War came into sight, and the awesome tasks of reconstruction and reconciliation loomed, Lincoln's deep heart's desire was a minimum of hate. When Senator Charles Sumner of Massachusetts spoke of Jefferson Davis—"Do not allow him to escape the law—he must be hanged"—Lincoln replied calmly, "Judge not, that ye be not judged." Again, as Sumner later wrote of it, he pressed Lincoln with a remark that the sight of Libby Prison made it impossible to pardon the President of the Confederate States, and Lincoln repeated twice over the words, "Judge not, that ye be not judged."

In his message of December 1, 1862, Lincoln told Congress of the need for action by the present and living generation, the territory of a nation, its land, being the only part which is of certain durability; and quoting from Scripture, he said: "One generation passeth away, and another generation cometh, but the earth abideth forever."

In Springfield, in the year 1858, biblical in color was Lincoln's address which ever thereafter was known as The House Divided speech. He quoted, "A house divided against itself cannot stand," adding, "I believe this Government cannot endure permanently half slave and half free." The brevity and portent of a Bible verse was there in the opening sentence of that speech:

"If we could first know where we are and whither we are tending, we could better judge what to do and how to do it."

The odor of true sanctity and an air of consecration past words saturates the letter of Lincoln to Mrs. Lydia Bixby of Boston, who had lost four sons in the war:

> But I cannot refrain from tendering to you the consolation that may be found in the thanks of the Republic they died to save. I pray that our Heavenly Father may assuage the anguish of your bereavement, and leave you only the cherished memory of the loved and lost, and the solemn pride that must be yours to have laid so costly a sacrifice upon the altar of Freedom.

The secretaries Nicolay and Hay were amazed at one instance of Lincoln's familiarity with the Bible. In 1864 news had come of the Cleveland, Ohio, convention of a third party which nominated John C. Frémont for President. A friend drifted into the White House, gave Lincoln an account of the convention, and said that instead of the many thousands expected there were present at no time more than 400 people. The President, struck by the number mentioned, reached for the Bible on his desk, searched a moment, then read the words: " 'And everyone that was in distress, and everyone that was in debt, and everyone that was discontented, gathered themselves unto him; and he became captain over them; and there were with him about four hundred men.' "

In proclamations, in recommendations of thanksgiving or of fasting and prayer, and in numerous references to God, Providence, the Almighty, the Common Father, Lincoln gave the impression to the multitude that he had a creed. A clergyman—William E. Barton—sought to formulate such a statement of faith from Lincoln's own words, changing the text merely to the extent of transposing pronouns from plural to singular, making other slight modifications, and prefixing the words, "I believe." The result was almost liturgical, containing expressions such as these:

I believe in penitential and pious sentiments, in devotional designs and purposes, in homages and confessions, in supplications to the Almighty, solemnly, earnestly, reverently.

I believe in blessings and comfort from the Father of Mercies to the sick, the wounded, the prisoners, and to the orphans and widows.

I believe it pleases Almighty God to prolong our national life, defending us with His guardian care.

I believe in His eternal truth and justice.

I believe the will of God prevails; without Him all human reliance is vain; without the assistance of that Divine Being I cannot succeed; with that assistance I cannot fail.

I believe I am a humble instrument in the hands of our Heavenly Father; I desire that all my works and acts may be according to His will; and that it may be so, I give thanks to the Almighty and seek His aid.

I believe in praise to Almighty God, the beneficent Creator and Ruler of the Universe.

Henry C. Deming, Congressman from Connecticut, reported that when Lincoln was asked why, with his obvious interest in religious matters and his familiarity with the Bible, he did not join a church, Lincoln replied:

When any church will inscribe over its altars, as its sole qualification for membership, the Savior's condensed statement for the substance of both law and gospel, "Thou shalt love the Lord thy God with all thy heart, and with all thy soul, and with all thy mind, and thy neighbor as thyself," that church will I join with all my heart and soul.

And his law partner, William H. Herndon, quotes Lincoln as saying that his religion was like that of an old man he once heard speak at a church meeting: "When I do good," the man had said, "I feel good; when I do bad, I feel bad; and that's my religion."

Although the Lincoln field has been worked and winnowed year after year, from time to time, happily enough, something new does turn up. It was not until some eighty years after his death that a printed statement was discovered in which he answered election campaign charges that he was "an open scoffer at Christianity" by saying, in part, "I have never denied the truth of the Scripture" and "I do not think I could myself, be brought to support a man for office whom I knew to be an open enemy of, and scoffer at, religion."

John Jay, grandson of the great Chief Justice and a notable Civil War figure himself, was reported by Frank B. Carpenter as saying he had seen Lincoln reading a "pocket edition of the New Testament." Cautious students have not accepted fully the report by Jay and others, due primarily to the lack of the Testament itself. Perhaps the discovery of this little book will increase research into the religious attitudes of Abraham Lincoln and throw new light on that long debated problem. In the meantime, some may ask themselves if the reported pocket Testament might not indeed have been this little devotional.

In "The Believer's Daily Treasure" Lincoln could come upon many sentences and phrases famous, important and often quoted; and many of the passages in the book could have had special interest for him, and direct or indirect influence on his thought and speech. This daily devotional, unseen for many years, takes us no farther toward placing Lincoln within creed or denomination; but it is new testimony that he was a man of profound faith. "Take all this book upon reason that you can, and the balance on faith," Lincoln said of the Bible to his friend Joshua Speed in 1864, "and you will live and die a better man."

—CARL SANDBURG

The devotional portion of this volume contains the entire text of "The Believer's Daily Treasure; or, Texts of Scripture Arranged for Every Day in the Year," published in 1852 by the Religious Tract Society of London, England. The material is reprinted as it appears in the copy of the book which Abraham Lincoln owned, and therefore contains the several inconsistencies and typographical errors found in the original edition.

THE
BELIEVER'S
DAILY
TREASURE;

or,

Texts of Scripture,
arranged for every day in the year.

The law of thy mouth is better unto me
than thousands of gold and silver.
Psalm cxix. 72.

FOURTH EDITION

LONDON:

THE RELIGIOUS TRACT SOCIETY;

Depository, 56, Paternoster Row, and
65, St. Paul's Churchyard;

AND SOLD BY THE BOOKSELLERS.

1852.

Contents

CONTENTS

CONTENTS

JANUARY

The True Believer

The Believer the Object of Divine Love

In this was manifested the love of God toward us, because that God sent his only begotten Son into the world, that we might live through him. *1 John iv. 9.*

> Pause, my soul, adore and wonder,
>   Ask, Oh, why such love to me?
> Grace hath put me in the number
>   Of the Saviour's family:
>   Hallelujah!
>   Thanks, eternal thanks to thee.

2

Redeemed by the Blood of Christ

Forasmuch as ye know that ye were not redeemed with corruptible things, as silver and gold—but with the precious blood of Christ, as of a lamb without blemish and without spot. *1 Pet. i. 18, 19.*

Our sins and griefs on him were laid;
    He meekly bore the mighty load:
Our ransom price he fully paid,
    By offering up himself to God.

3

Renewed by the Holy Ghost

Not by works of righteousness which we have done, but according to his mercy he saved us, by the washing of regeneration, and renewing of the Holy Ghost.
Titus iii. 5.

Vain is every outward rite,
    Unless thy grace be given:
Nothing but thy life and light,
    Can form a soul for heaven.

4

Partaker of the Divine Nature

Whereby are given unto us exceeding great and precious promises: that by these ye might be partakers of the divine nature, having escaped the corruption that is in the world through lust. *2 Pet. i. 4.*

> Blessed are the sons of God;
> They are bought with Christ's own blood;
> They produce the fruits of grace
> In the works of righteousness:
> Born of God, they hate all sin;
> God's pure word remains within.

5

Justified Before God Through Christ

By him all that believe are justified from all things, from which ye could not be justified by the law of Moses. *Acts xiii. 39.*

> Jesus, thy blood and righteousness
> My beauty are, and glorious dress;
> 'Midst flaming worlds, in these array'd,
> With joy shall I lift up my head.

6

United to Christ

I am the vine, ye are the branches: he that abideth in me, and I in him, the same bringeth forth much fruit: for without me ye can do nothing. *John xv. 5.*

Lord of the vineyard, we adore
That power and grace divine,
Which plants our wild, our barren souls,
In Christ the living Vine.

For ever there may I abide,
And from that vital root,
Be influence spread through every branch,
To form and feed the fruit.

7

Joint-Heir with Christ

If children, then heirs; heirs of God, and joint-heirs with Christ. *Rom. viii. 17.*

Pronounce me, gracious God, thy son;
Own me an heir divine;
I'll pity princes on the throne,
When I can call thee mine:
Sceptres and crowns unenvied rise,
And lose their lustre in mine eyes.

8

Complete in Christ

For in him dwelleth all the fulness of the Godhead
bodily. And ye are complete in him. *Col. ii. 9, 10.*

> Thy saints on earth, and those above,
>   Here join in sweet accord:
> One body all in mutual love,
>   And thou their common Lord.
> Yes, thou that body wilt present
>   Before thy Father's face,
> Nor shall a wrinkle or a spot
>   Its beauteous form disgrace.

9

Christ the Believer's Advocate

If any man sin, we have an advocate with the Father,
Jesus Christ the righteous. *1 John ii. 1.*

> Look up, my soul, with cheerful eye,
>   See where the great Redeemer stands—
> Thy glorious Advocate on high,
>   With precious incense in his hands.
>
> He sweetens every humble groan,
>   He recommends each broken prayer;
> Recline thy hope on him alone,
>   Whose power and love forbid despair.

10

Christ the Hope of the Believer

Paul, an apostle of Jesus Christ by the commandment of God our Saviour, and Lord Jesus Christ, which is our hope. *1 Tim. i. 1.*

> Jesus, my Lord, I look to thee;
>> Where else can helpless sinners go?
> Thy boundless love shall set me free
>> From all my wretchedness and woe.

11

Christ the Life of the Believer

When Christ, who is our life, shall appear, then shall ye also appear with him in glory. *Col. iii. 4.*

> If my immortal Saviour lives,
>> Then my eternal life is sure;
> His word a firm foundation gives,
>> Here let me build, and rest secure.

> Here, O my soul, thy trust repose;
>> If Jesus is for ever mine,
> Not death itself, that last of foes,
>> Shall break a union so divine.

12

Christ the Peace of the Believer

Now in Christ Jesus ye who sometime were far off are made nigh by the blood of Christ. For he is our peace.
Eph. ii. 13, 14.

"He is our peace"—for by his blood
Sinners are reconcil'd to God;
Sweet harmony is now restor'd,
And man beloved, and God ador'd.

13

Christ the Righteousness of the Believer

This is his name whereby he shall be called, The Lord our righteousness. *Jer. xxiii. 6.*

Saviour divine, we know thy name,
    And in that name we trust;
Thou art the Lord our righteousness,
    Thou art thine Israel's boast.

That spotless robe which thou hast wrought,
    Shall clothe us all around,
Nor by the piercing eye of God
    One blemish shall be found.

14

The Temple of the Spirit

Know ye not that your body is the temple of the Holy
Ghost which is in you, which ye have of God.

1 Cor. vi. 19.

Creator Spirit! by whose aid
The world's foundations first were laid,
Come, visit every humble mind;
Come, pour thy joys on human kind:
From sin and sorrow set us free,
And make us temples worthy thee.

15

Sanctified by the Spirit

God hath from the beginning chosen you to salvation
through sanctification of the Spirit and belief of the
truth. *2 Thess. ii. 13.*

Come, Holy Spirit, love divine,
Thy cleansing power impart;
Each erring thought and wish refine
That wanders near my heart.

16

Upheld by the Spirit

That he would grant you, according to the riches of his glory, to be strengthened with might by his Spirit in the inner man. *Eph. iii. 16.*

> Assisted by his grace,
>   We still pursue our way;
> And hope at last to reach the prize,
>   Secure in endless day.

17

The Spirit of Adoption Received

Ye have not received the spirit of bondage again to fear; but ye have received the Spirit of adoption, whereby we cry, Abba, Father. *Rom. viii. 15.*

> Assure my conscience of her part
>   In the Redeemer's blood,
> And bear thy witness in my heart
>   That I am born of God.

18

Comforted by the Spirit

When the Comforter is come, whom I will send unto you from the Father, even the Spirit of truth, which proceedeth from the Father, he shall testify of me.

John xv. 26.

In the hour of my distress,
When temptations me oppress,
And when I my sins confess—
    Sweet Spirit, comfort me.

19

Sealed by the Spirit

Grieve not the holy Spirit of God, whereby ye are sealed unto the day of redemption. *Eph. iv. 30.*

Forbid it, Lord, that we
Who from thy hands receive
The Spirit's power to make us free,
    Should e'er that Spirit grieve.

O keep our faith alive,
Help us to watch and pray;
Lest, by our carelessness, we drive
    The sacred Guest away.

20

Taught by the Spirit

When he, the Spirit of truth, is come, he will guide you into all truth: for he shall not speak of himself; but whatsoever he shall hear, that shall he speak: and he will show you things to come. *John xvi. 13.*

> Thine inward teachings make me know
>> The mysteries of redeeming love,
> The emptiness of things below,
>> And excellence of things above.

21

Fellow-Citizen with the Saints

Now therefore ye are no more strangers and foreigners, but fellow-citizens with the saints, and of the household of God. *Eph. ii. 19.*

> The kindred links of life are bright,
>> Yet not so bright as those
> In which Christ's favoured friends unite,
>> And each on each repose:
> Where all the hearts in union cling,
> With Him, the centre and the spring.

22

Lives a Life of Faith in Christ

I am crucified with Christ: nevertheless I live; yet not I, but Christ liveth in me: and the life which I now live in the flesh I live by the faith of the Son of God.

Gal. ii. 20.

Close to the ignominious tree,
    Jesus, my humbled soul would cleave;
Despised and crucified with thee,
    With Christ resolved to die and live:
There would I bow my suppliant knee,
And own no other Lord but thee.

23

Lives a Life of Consecration to God

I beseech you therefore, brethren, by the mercies of God, that ye present your bodies a living sacrifice, holy, acceptable unto God, which is your reasonable service. *Rom. xii.* 1.

Thine, wholly thine, I want to be;
    The sacrifice receive:
Made, and preserved, and saved by thee,
    To thee myself I give.

24

Lives a Life of Hope

Looking for the mercy of our Lord Jesus Christ unto eternal life. *Jude 21*.

Rejoice in glorious hope;
     Jesus, the Judge, shall come,
And take his servants up
     To their eternal home:
Lift up your heart, lift up your voice;
Rejoice, he bids his saints rejoice.

25

Delivered from Condemnation

There is now no condemnation to them which are in Christ Jesus, who walk not after the flesh, but after the Spirit. *Rom. viii. 1*.

O Love, thou bottomless abyss!
     My sins are swallow'd up in thee;
Cover'd is my unrighteousness,
     From condemnation now I'm free;
While Jesus' blood through earth and skies,
"Mercy, free boundless mercy!" cries.

26

Delivered from the Power of Satan

Forasmuch then as the children are partakers of flesh
and blood, he also himself likewise took part of the
same; that through death he might destroy him that
had the power of death, that is, the devil. *Heb. ii. 14.*

> Dry up your tears, ye saints, and tell
>> How high your great Deliverer reigns;
> Sing, how he spoiled the host of hell,
>> And led the tyrant Death in chains.

27

Delivered from All Iniquity

Let Israel hope in the Lord: for with the Lord there is
mercy, and with him is plenteous redemption. And
he shall redeem Israel from all his iniquities.

Psalm cxxx. 7, 8.

> Fix'd on this ground will I remain,
>> Though my heart fail, and flesh decay;
> This anchor shall my soul sustain,
>> When earth's foundations melt away:
> Mercy's full power I then shall prove,
> Lov'd with an everlasting love.

28

Delivered from All Enemies

He delivereth me from mine enemies; yea, thou liftest me above those that rise up against me. *Psalm xviii. 48.*

Foes are round us, but we stand
On the borders of our land:
Jesus, God's exalted Son,
Bids us undismay'd go on:
Onward then we gladly press
Through this earthly wilderness.

29

Enjoys a Present Salvation

Which in time past were not a people, but are now the people of God: which had not obtained mercy, but now have obtained mercy. *1 Pet. ii. 10.*

Fill'd with holy emulation
   Let us vie with those above:
Sweet the theme—a free salvation,
   Fruit of everlasting love.

30

Preserved unto Eternal Salvation

Who are kept by the power of God through faith unto salvation ready to be revealed in the last time.

1 Pet. 1. 5.

Saints by the power of God are kept
Till full salvation come;
We walk by faith as strangers here
Till Christ shall call us home.

31

A Pilgrim to a Heavenly Country

Now they desire a better country, that is, an heavenly: wherefore God is not ashamed to be called their God: for he hath prepared for them a city. *Heb. xi. 16.*

'Tis true, we are but strangers
And sojourners below;
And countless snares and dangers
Surround the path we go:
Though painful and distressing,
Yet there's a rest above,
And onward we are pressing
To reach that land of love.

FEBRUARY

Evidences of
the Believer

I

Supreme Love to God

Master, what shall I do to inherit eternal life?—And he
answering said, Thou shalt love the Lord thy God with
all thy heart, and with all thy soul, and with all thy
strength, and with all thy mind. *Luke x. 25, 27.*

> Yes, I would love thee, blessed God!
>   Paternal goodness marks thy name;
> Thy praises, through thy high abode,
>   The heavenly hosts with joy proclaim.

2

Gratitude to God

And one of them, [the ten lepers,] when he saw that he was healed, turned back, and with a loud voice glorified God. *Luke xvii. 15.*

> What thanks I owe thee, and what love,
>   A boundless, endless store,
> Shall echo through the realms above,
>   When time shall be no more.

3

Obedience to God

Ye were the servants of sin, but ye have obeyed from the heart that form of doctrine which was delivered you. Being then made free from sin, ye became the servants of righteousness. *Rom. vi. 17, 18.*

> Love is the fountain whence
>   All true obedience flows;
> The Christian serves the God he loves,
>   And loves the God he knows.

4

Submission to God

We have had fathers of our flesh which corrected us, and we gave them reverence: shall we not much rather be in subjection unto the Father of spirits, and live? *Heb. xii.* 9.

Oh let my trembling soul be still,
　　While darkness veils this mortal eye,
And wait thy wise, thy holy will
　　Wrapp'd yet in tears and mystery:
I cannot, Lord, thy purpose see,
Yet all is well—since ruled by thee.

5

Faith in Christ

Whosoever believeth that Jesus is the Christ is born of God. *1 John v.* 1.

Lord, I believe thy heavenly word;
Fain would I have my soul renew'd;
I mourn for sin, and trust the Lord
To have it pardon'd and subdued.

O may thy grace its power display,
Let guilt and death no longer reign;
Save me in thine appointed way,
Nor let my humble faith be vain.

6

Love to Christ

He that loveth father or mother more than me is not
worthy of me: and he that loveth son or daughter more
than me is not worthy of me. *Matt. x. 37.*

> Whom have I on earth below?
> Thee, and only thee, I know:
> Whom have I in heaven but thee?
> Thou art all in all to me.

7

Self-Denial for Christ

If any man will come after me, let him deny himself,
and take up his cross daily, and follow me. *Luke ix. 23.*

> Take up thy cross, let not its weight
>   Fill thy weak spirit with alarm,
> My strength shall bear thy spirit up,
>   And brace thy heart, and nerve thy arm.

> Take up thy cross, and follow me,
>   Nor think till death to lay it down;
> For only he who bears the cross
>   May hope to wear the glorious crown.

8

Confession of Christ

Whosoever shall confess that Jesus is the Son of God, God dwelleth in him, and he in God. *1 John iv. 15.*

> I'll tell to all poor sinners round,
> How great a Saviour I have found;
> I'll point to his redeeming blood,
> And say, "Behold the way to God."

9

Devotedness to Christ

For whether we live, we live unto the Lord; and whether we die, we die unto the Lord: whether we live therefore, or die, we are the Lord's. *Rom. xiv. 8.*

> My soul, and all its powers,
>   Thine, wholly thine, shall be;
> All, all my happy hours
>   I consecrate to thee:
> Whate'er I have, whate'er I am,
> Shall magnify my Saviour's name.

10

Imitation of Christ

For I have given you an example, that ye should do as
I have done to you. *John xiii. 15.*

> Thy fair example may I trace,
> To teach me what I ought to be:
> Make me, by thy transforming grace,
> My Saviour, daily more like thee.

11

Christ Is Precious

Behold, I lay in Sion a chief corner stone, elect, precious: and he that believeth on him shall not be confounded. Unto you therefore which believe he is
precious. *1 Pet. ii. 6, 7.*

> Jesus, in thy transporting name
> What glories meet our eyes!
> Thou art the angels' sweetest theme,
> The wonder of the skies.

> Oh may our willing hearts confess
> Thy sweet, thy gentle sway;
> Glad captives of thy matchless grace,
> Thy righteous rule obey.

12

Possession of the Spirit of Christ

Ye are not in the flesh, but in the Spirit, if so be that the Spirit of God dwell in you. Now if any man have not the Spirit of Christ, he is none of his. *Rom. viii. 9.*

Author of our new creation,
    Let us all thine influence prove;
Make our souls thy habitation;
    Shed abroad the Saviour's love.

13

Led by the Spirit

For as many as are led by the Spirit of God, they are the sons of God. *Rom. viii. 14.*

Lead us to holiness—the road
That we must take to dwell with God:
Lead us to Christ—the living way,
Nor let us from his pastures stray:
Lead us to God—our final rest,
In his enjoyment to be blest:
Lead us to heaven—the seat of bliss,
Where pleasure in perfection is.

14

Conviction of Sin

There is no soundness in my flesh because of thine anger; neither is there any rest in my bones because of my sin. For mine iniquities are gone over mine head: as an heavy burden they are too heavy for me.

Psalm xxxviii. 3, 4.

O Thou that hear'st the prayer of faith,
Wilt thou not save my soul from death,
  My soul that rests on thee?
I have no refuge of my own,
But fly to what my Lord hath done
  And suffer'd once for me.

15

Repentance for Sin

Godly sorrow worketh repentance to salvation not to be repented of: but the sorrow of the world worketh death. *2 Cor. vii. 10.*

My lips with shame my sins confess
Against thy law, against thy grace:
Lo, should thy judgments grow severe,
I am condemn'd, but thou art clear.

16

Hatred to Sin

Whosoever is born of God doth not commit sin; for his seed remaineth in him: and he cannot sin, because he is born of God. *1 John iii. 9.*

> Oh! give me, Lord, the tender heart
> That trembles at the' approach of sin,
> A godly fear of sin impart,
> Implant and root it deep within.

17

Mortification of Sin

They that are Christ's have crucified the flesh with the affections and lusts. *Gal. v. 24.*

> Great God, assist me through the fight;
> Make me triumphant in thy might:
> Thou the desponding heart canst raise;
> The victory mine, and thine the praise.

18

Self-Righteousness Renounced

Yea doubtless, and I count all things but loss for the excellency of the knowledge of Christ Jesus my Lord: for whom I have suffered the loss of all things, and do count them but dung, that I may win Christ. *Phil. iii. 8.*

> On thee alone my hope relies;
>   Beneath the cross I fall,
> My Lord, my life, my sacrifice,
>   My Saviour, and my all.

19

The World Overcome by Faith

Whatsoever is born of God overcometh the world: and this is the victory that overcometh the world, even our faith. *1 John v. 4.*

> 'Tis faith that conquers earth and hell
>   By a celestial power;
> This is the grace that shall prevail
>   In the decisive hour.

20

Non-Conformity to the World

Love not the world, neither the things that are in the world. If any man love the world, the love of the Father is not in him. *1 John ii. 15.*

Why should our poor enjoyments here
Be thought so pleasant and so dear,
    And tempt our hearts astray?
Our brightest joys are fading fast,
The longest life will soon be past;
And if we go to heaven at last,
    We need not wish to stay.

21

Spiritual-Mindedness

They that are after the flesh do mind the things of the flesh; but they that are after the Spirit the things of the Spirit. *Rom. viii. 5.*

Let worldly minds the world pursue,
    It has no charms for me;
Once I admired its trifles too,
    But grace has set me free.

22

Heavenly-Mindedness

Our conversation is in heaven; from whence also we look for the Saviour, the Lord Jesus Christ. *Phil. iii. 20.*

> Beyond the bounds of time and space
> Look forward to that heavenly place,
>   The saints' secure abode;
> On faith's strong eagle pinion rise,
> And force your passage to the skies,
>   Strong in the strength of God.

23

Constrained by Love

The love of Christ constraineth us; because we thus judge, that if one died for all, then were all dead: and that he died for all, that they which live should not henceforth live unto themselves, but unto him which died for them, and rose again. *2 Cor. v. 14, 15.*

> Be all my heart, be all my days,
> Devoted to thy single praise;
> And let my glad obedience prove
> How much I owe, how much I love.

24

Love of the Truth

We are of God: he that knoweth God heareth us; he
that is not of God heareth not us. Hereby know we the
spirit of truth, and the spirit of error. *1 John iv. 6.*

Order my footsteps by thy word,
  And make my heart sincere;
Let sin have no dominion, Lord,
  But keep my conscience clear.

25

Perseverance in the Truth

They went out from us, but they were not of us; for if
they had been of us, they would no doubt have contin-
ued with us: but they went out, that they might be
made manifest that they were not all of us. *1 John ii. 19.*

When any turn from Zion's way,
  (Alas, what numbers do!)
Methinks I hear my Saviour say,
  Wilt thou forsake me too?

26

Love to the Scriptures

I love thy commandments above gold; yea, above fine gold. Thy testimonies are wonderful: therefore doth my soul keep them. *Ps. cxix. 127, 129.*

> Here mines of knowledge, love, and joy,
>   Are open'd to our sight,
> The purest gold without alloy,
>   And gems divinely bright.

27

Love to Enemies

Love ye your enemies, and do good, and lend, hoping for nothing again; and your reward shall be great, and ye shall be the children of the Highest: for he is kind unto the unthankful and to the evil. *Luke vi. 3.*

> Lord, shall thy bright example shine
>   In vain before my eyes?
> Give me a soul akin to thine,
>   To love my enemies.

28

Love to the Brethren

Beloved, let us love one another: for love is of God; and every one that loveth is born of God, and knoweth God. *1 John iv. 7.*

> Bless'd be the tie that binds
> Our hearts in Christian love;
> The fellowship of kindred minds
> Is like to that above.

29 {Leap Year}

The Witness of Conscience

Hereby we know that we are of the truth, and shall assure our hearts before him. Beloved, if our heart condemn us not, then have we confidence toward God.

1 John iii. 19, 21.

> How happy are the new-born race,
> Partakers of adopting grace!
>   How pure the bliss they share!
> Hid from the world and all its eyes,
> Within their hearts the blessing lies,
>   And conscience feels it there.

MARCH

Privileges of the Believer

I

God the Believer's Sun and Shield

The Lord God is a sun and shield: the Lord will give grace and glory; no good thing will he withhold from them that walk uprightly. *Ps. lxxxiv. 11.*

If thou art my shield and my sun,
   The night is no darkness to me;
And fast as my moments roll on,
   They bring me but nearer to thee.

2
God the Portion of the Believer

God is the strength of my heart, and my portion for ever. *Ps. lxxiii. 26.*

> His boundless grace shall all my need supply,
> When streams of creature-comfort cease to
>   flow:
> And should he some inferior good deny,
> 'Tis but a greater blessing to bestow.

3
God the Refuge of the Believer

God is our refuge and strength, a very present help in trouble. Therefore will not we fear, though the earth be removed, and though the mountains be carried into the midst of the sea. *Psa. xlvi. 1, 2.*

> God is our refuge in distress,
> A present help when dangers press;
>   In him undaunted I'll confide,
> Though earth were from her centre toss'd,
> And mountains in the ocean lost,
>   Torn piece-meal by the roaring tide.

{ 33 }

4

God the Guide of the Believer

This God is our God for ever and ever: he will be our guide even unto death. *Ps. xlviii. 14.*

Haste thee on from grace to glory,
　Arm'd by faith, and wing'd by prayer;
Heaven's eternal day's before thee,
　God's own hand shall guide thee there.

5

God the Glory of the Believer

Thou, Lord, art a shield for me; my glory, and the lifter up of mine head. *Ps. iii. 3.*

Lord, let thy grace surround me still,
　And like a bulwark prove,
To guard my soul from every ill,
　Secured by sovereign love.

6

All Blessings Through Christ

All things are yours; whether Paul, or Apollos, or
Cephas, or the world, or life, or death, or things
present, or things to come; all are yours; and ye are
Christ's; and Christ is God's. *1 Cor. iii.* 21–23.

> Let Christ assure me he is mine,
>   I nothing want beside;
> My soul shall at the fountain live,
>   When all the streams are dried.

7

All Blessings in Christ

Blessed be the God and Father of our Lord Jesus
Christ, who hath blessed us with all spiritual blessings
in heavenly places in Christ Jesus. *Eph. i.* 3.

> Oh the rich depths of love divine!
>   Of bliss a boundless store!
> Dear Saviour, let me call thee mine,
>   I cannot wish for more.

8

Pardon Through Christ

In whom we have redemption through his blood, even
the forgiveness of sin. *Col. i. 14.*

> O Lamb of God, thy precious blood
>   Shall never lose its power,
> Till all the ransom'd church of God
>   Is saved, to sin no more.
>
> E'er since, by faith, I saw the stream
>   Thy flowing wounds supply,
> Redeeming love has been my theme,
>   And shall be till I die.

9

Justification Through Christ

Being justified freely by his grace through the
redemption that is in Christ Jesus. *Rom. iii. 24.*

> No righteousness but his we own,
> No ransom but his blood alone:
> While on the Father's name we call,
> Our faith pleads Christ as all in all.

10

Reconciliation Through Christ

For if, when we were enemies, we were reconciled to God by the death of his Son, much more, being reconciled, we shall be saved by his life. *Rom. v. 10.*

Let us love, and sing, and wonder;
　　Let us praise the Saviour's name:
He has hush'd the law's loud thunder,
　　He has quench'd Mount Sinai's flame:
He has wash'd us with his blood,
He has brought us nigh to God.

11

Adoption Through Christ

As many as received him, to them gave he power to become the sons of God, even to them that believe on his name. *John i. 12.*

Let others boast their ancient line,
　　In long succession great;
In the proud list, let heroes shine
　　And monarchs swell their state:
Descended from the King of kings,
Each saint a nobler title sings.

12

Rest in Christ

Come unto me, all ye that labour and are heavy laden,
and I will give you rest. *Matt. xi. 28.*

Jesus, with thy word complying,
    Firm our faith and hope shall be;
On thy faithfulness relying,
    We will seek our rest in thee.

13

Safety in Christ

I give unto them eternal life; and they shall never perish, neither shall any man pluck them out of my hand.
John x. 28.

"Unnumber'd years of bliss
    I to my sheep will give;
And while my throne unshaken stands
    Shall all my chosen live."

Enough, my gracious Lord,
    Let faith triumphant cry;
My heart can on this promise live,
    Can with this promise die.

14

Strength Through Christ

I can do all things through Christ which strengtheneth
me. *Phil. iv. 13.*

> I can do all things, and can bear
> All sufferings, if my Lord be near;
> Sweet pleasures mingle with the pains,
> While his left hand my head sustains.

15

Spiritual Freedom Through Christ

If the Son shall make you free, ye shall be free indeed.
John viii. 36.

> Sweet is the freedom Christ bestows,
> With which he makes his people free,
> A liberty no mortal knows
> Till they his great salvation see.

16

Consolation Through Christ

Now our Lord Jesus Christ himself, and God, even our Father, which hath loved us, and hath given us everlasting consolation and good hope through grace.

2 Thess. ii. 16.

In every trouble, sharp and strong,
  My soul to Jesus flies;
My anchor-hold is firm on him,
  When swelling billows rise.

17

Peace with God Through Christ

Being justified by faith, we have peace with God through our Lord Jesus Christ. *Rom. v. 1.*

No fiery vengeance now,
  Nor burning wrath comes down;
If justice call for sinners' blood,
  The Saviour shows his own.

18

Access to God Through Christ

In whom we have boldness and access with confidence by the faith of him. *Eph. iii. 12.*

Come boldly to the throne of grace,
Where Jesus kindly pleads;
Our's cannot be a desperate case
While Jesus intercedes.

19

Victory Through Christ

Thanks be to God, which giveth us the victory through our Lord Jesus Christ. *1 Cor. xv. 57.*

Thus strong in the Redeemer's strength,
Sin, death, and hell we trample down,
Fight the good fight, and win at length,
Through mercy, an eternal crown.

20

Indwelling of the Spirit

Know ye not that ye are the temple of God, and that the Spirit of God dwelleth in you? *1 Cor. iii. 16.*

Think what Spirit dwells within thee;
Think what Father's smiles are thine;
Think that Jesus died to win thee:
Child of heaven, canst thou repine?

21

Intercession of the Spirit

The Spirit also helpeth our infirmities: for we know not what we should pray for as we ought: but the Spirit itself maketh intercession for us with groanings which cannot be uttered. *Rom. viii. 26.*

Let pure devotion's fervours rise,
Let every holy feeling glow;
Oh, let the rapture of the skies
Kindle in our cold hearts below.
Come, vivifying Spirit, come,
And make our hearts thy constant home.

22

Sanctification by the Spirit

Elect according to the foreknowledge of God the Father, through sanctification of the Spirit, unto obedience and sprinkling of the blood of Jesus. *1 Pet. i. 2.*

> Can aught beneath a power divine
>   The stubborn will subdue?
> 'Tis thine, eternal Spirit, thine,
>   To form our hearts anew.
> 'Tis thine the passions to recall,
>   And upwards bid them rise;
> And make the scales of error fall
>   From reason's darkened eyes.

23

The Fruits of the Spirit

The fruit of the Spirit is love, joy, peace, long-suffering, gentleness, goodness, faith, meekness, temperance: against such there is no law. *Gal. v. 22, 23.*

> 'Tis God himself the ground prepares,
>   His Spirit sows the land;
> And every pleasant fruit it bears,
>   Is nurtur'd by his hand.

{ 43 }

24

Inheritance Among the Sanctified

Brethren, I commend you to God, and to the word of his grace, which is able to build you up, and to give you an inheritance among all them which are sanctified. *Acts xx. 32.*

From earth we shall quickly remove,
   And mount to our native abode;
The house of our Father above,
   The palace of angels and God.

25

Increase of Grace

The righteous shall flourish like the palm tree: he shall grow like a cedar in Lebanon. They shall still bring forth fruit in old age; they shall be fat and flourishing.
Ps. xcii. 12, 14.

Lord, one thing we want,
   More holiness grant;
For more of thy mind and thy image we pant:
   While onward we move
   To Canaan above,
Come, fill us with holiness, fill us with love.

26

Persevering Grace

The righteous shall hold on his way, and he that hath clean hands shall be stronger and stronger. *Job xvii. 9.*

> The righteous, bless'd with light divine,
> Shall prosper on their way;
> Brighter and brighter still shall shine,
> To glory's perfect day.

27

Confidence in Prayer

This is the confidence that we have in him, that, if we ask any thing according to his will, he heareth us.

1 John v. 14.

> He who for man their Surety stood,
> And poured on earth his precious blood,
> Pursues in heaven his mighty plan,
> The Saviour and the friend of man.
>
> With boldness, therefore, at the throne,
> Let us make all our sorrows known;
> And ask the aid of heavenly power,
> To help us in the evil hour.

28

Preservation in Trouble

In the time of trouble he shall hide me in his pavilion:
in the secret of his tabernacle shall he hide me; he shall
set me upon a rock. *Ps. xxvii. 5.*

> When I can trust my all with God,
>   In trial's fearful hour—
> Bow, all resign'd, beneath his rod,
>   And bless his sparing power;
> A joy springs up amid distress,
> A fountain in the wilderness.

29

All Things Work Together for Good

We know that all things work together for good to
them that love God, to them who are the called
according to his purpose. *Rom. viii. 28.*

> God will keep his own anointed;
>   Nought shall harm them, none condemn;
> All their trials are appointed;
>   All must work for good to them:
>   All shall help them
>   To their heavenly diadem.

30

Peace of Mind

Thou wilt keep him in perfect peace, whose mind is stayed on thee: because he trusteth in thee. *Isa. xxvi. 3.*

> Saviour, on earth I covet not
>   That every woe should cease;
> Only, if trouble be my lot,
>   In thee let me have peace.

31

Peace in Death

Mark the perfect man, and behold the upright: for the end of that man is peace. *Ps. xxxvii. 37.*

> How bless'd the righteous when he dies,
>   When sinks a weary soul to rest!
> How mildly beam the closing eyes!
>   How gently heaves the' expiring breast!
>
> Life's labour done, as sinks the clay,
>   Light from its load the spirit flies;
> While heaven and earth combine to say,
>   "How bless'd the righteous when he dies!"

APRIL

Duties of the Believer—Personal

I
Good Works to Be Done

These things I will that thou affirm constantly, that they which have believed in God might be careful to maintain good works. *Titus iii. 8.*

Whate'er is noble, pure, refined,
Just, generous, amiable, and kind,
That may my constant thoughts pursue,
That may I love and practise too.

2

Good Works to Be Done to the Glory of God

Whether therefore ye eat, or drink, or whatsoever ye do, do all to the glory of God. *1 Cor. x. 31.*

> Through Jesus Christ the Just,
>   My faint desires receive;
> And let me in thy goodness trust,
>   And to thy glory live.

3

Good Works to Be Done After the Example of Christ

He that saith he abideth in him ought himself also so to walk, even as he walked. *1 John ii. 6.*

> To do his heavenly Father's will
>   Was his employment and delight;
> Humility and holy zeal
>   Shone through his life divinely bright.

4

Good Works to Be Done
Through the Grace of Christ

Now the God of peace make you perfect in every good work to do his will, working in you that which is well pleasing in his sight, through Jesus Christ; to whom be glory for ever and ever. *Heb. xiii. 20, 21.*

> Then shall we do, with pure delight,
> Whate'er is pleasing in thy sight,
>   As vessels of thy richest grace;
> And, having thy whole counsel done,
> To thee and thy co-equal Son
>   Ascribe the everlasting praise.

5

Good Works to Be Done
in the Name of Christ

Whatsoever ye do in word or deed, do all in the name of the Lord Jesus, giving thanks to God and the Father by him. *Col. iii. 17.*

> Whate'er I say or do,
>   Thy glory be my aim;
> My offerings all be offered through
>   His ever blessed name.

6

Improvement of Time

Knowing the time, that now it is high time to awake out of sleep: for now is our salvation nearer than when we believed. *Rom. xiii. 11.*

> The time is short, but who can tell
> How short his time below may be?
> To-day on earth his soul may dwell,
> To-morrow in eternity.

7

Improvement of Privileges

That on the good ground are they, which in an honest and good heart, having heard the word, keep it, and bring forth fruit with patience. *Luke vii. 15.*

> Father of mercies, we have need
> Of thy preparing grace;
> Let the same hand that gives the seed
> Provide a fruitful place.

8

Improvement of Opportunities

Whatsoever thy hand findeth to do, do it with thy might; for there is no work, nor device, nor knowledge, nor wisdom, in the grave, whither thou goest.

Eccles. ix. 10.

Whate'er our hands shall find to do,
    To-day may we with zeal pursue;
Seize fleeting moments as they fly,
    And live as we would wish to die.

9

Spiritual Diligence

This one thing I do, forgetting those things which are behind, and reaching forth unto those things which are before, I press toward the mark for the prize of the high calling of God in Christ Jesus. *Phil. iii. 13, 14.*

A scrip on my back, and a staff in my hand,
I march on in haste through an enemy's land:
The road may be rough, but it cannot be long,
So I'll smooth it with hope, and I'll cheer it
    with song.

10

Entire Consecration

Neither yield ye your members as instruments of unrighteousness unto sin: but yield yourselves unto God, as those that are alive from the dead, and your members as instruments of righteousness unto God.

Rom. vi. 13.

Yield to the Lord, with simple heart,
All that thou hast, and all thou art:
Renounce all strength, but strength divine,
And peace shall be for ever thine.

11

Open Profession of Christ

Whosoever shall confess me before men, him will I confess also before my Father which is in heaven.

Matt. x. 32.

Should I to gain the world's applause,
Or to escape its harmless frown,
Refuse to countenance thy cause,
And make thy people's lot my own,
What shame would fill me in that day,
When thou thy glory shalt display!

12

Evil Appearances to Be Avoided

Abstain from all appearance of evil. *1 Thess. v. 22.*

Our Saviour by a heavenly birth
Calls us to holiness on earth,
Bids us our former follies hate,
And from the wicked separate.

We must have holy hearts and hands,
And feet that go where he commands;
A holy will to keep his ways,
And holy lips to speak his praise.

13

Diligence in Keeping the Heart

Keep thy heart with all diligence; for out of it are the
issues of life. *Prov. iv. 23.*

Thy business be to keep thy heart,
    Each passion to control;
Nobly ambitious well to rule
    The empire of thy soul.

14

Search the Scriptures

Search the Scriptures; for in them ye think ye have
eternal life: and they are they which testify of me.

John v. 39.

Lord, thy teaching grace impart,
  That we may not read in vain;
Write thy precepts on our heart,
  Make thy truths and doctrine plain;
Let the message of thy love
Guide us to thy rest above.

15

Secret Prayer

Thou, when thou prayest, enter into thy closet, and
when thou hast shut thy door, pray to thy Father
which is in secret; and thy Father which seeth in secret
shall reward thee openly. *Matt. vi. 6.*

Far from the paths of men, to Thee
  I solemnly retire;
See Thou, who dost in secret see,
  And grant my heart's desire.

16

Thanksgiving

In every thing give thanks: for this is the will of God
in Christ Jesus concerning you. *1 Thess. v. 18.*

> Praise to God, immortal praise,
> For the love that crowns our days;
> Bounteous Source of every joy,
> Let thy praise our tongues employ.

17

Meditation

His delight is in the law of the Lord; and in his law
doth he meditate day and night. *Psalm i. 2.*

> I love in solitude to shed
> The penitential tear;
> And all his promises to plead,
> When none but God is near.
>
> I love to think on mercies past,
> And future good implore;
> And all my cares and sorrows cast
> On him whom I adore.

18

Self-Examination

Examine yourselves, whether ye be in the faith; prove your own selves. *2 Cor. xiii. 5.*

At evening to myself I say,
My soul, where hast thou glean'd to-day,
  Thy labours how bestow'd?
What hast thou rightly said or done?
What grace attain'd, or knowledge won,
  In following after God?

19

In Prosperity to Be Humble

For I say, through the grace given unto me, to every man that is among you, not to think of himself more highly than he ought to think. *Rom. xii. 3.*

Lord, if thou thy grace impart,
Poor in spirit, meek in heart,
I shall, as my Saviour, be
Rooted in humility:
Pleas'd with all the Lord provides,
Wean'd from all the world besides.

20

In Adversity to Trust God

Who is among you that feareth the Lord, that obeyeth
the voice of his servant, that walketh in darkness, and
hath no light? let him trust in the name of the Lord,
and stay upon his God. *Isa. l. 10.*

> If Providence our comforts shroud,
>   And dark distresses lower,
> Hope paints its rainbow on the cloud,
>   And grace shines through the shower.

21

Self-Government

He that is slow to anger is better than the mighty; and
he that ruleth his spirit than he that taketh a city.

Prov. xvi. 32.

> Happy the man, whose cautious steps
>   Still keep the golden mean;
> Whose life, by Scripture rules well form'd,
>   Declares a conscience clean.

22

Self-Denial

All things are lawful for me, but all things are not expedient: all things are lawful for me, but all things edify not. *1 Cor. x. 23*.

Lord, ever let me freely yield
What most I prize to thee,
Who never hast a good withheld,
Or wilt withhold from me.

Thy favour all my journey through,
Thou art engaged to grant;
What else I want, or think I do,
'Tis better still to want.

23

Contentment

Be content with such things as ye have: for he hath said, I will never leave thee, nor forsake thee. *Heb. xiii. 5*.

Since he has said "I'll ne'er depart,"
I'll bind his promise to my heart,
Rejoicing in his care:
This shall support while here I live,
And, when in glory I arrive,
Will praise him for it there.

24

Patience

Ye have need of patience, that, after ye have done the will of God, ye might receive the promise. *Heb. x. 36.*

I would submit to all thy will,
    For thou art good and wise;
Let every anxious thought be still,
    Nor one faint murmur rise.

Thy love can cheer the darksome gloom,
    And bid me wait serene,
Till hopes and joys immortal bloom
    And brighten all the scene.

25

Meekness

Walk worthy of the vocation wherewith ye are called, with all lowliness and meekness, with long suffering, forbearing one another in love. *Eph. iv. 2.*

Meekness, humility, and love,
    Did through thy conduct shine;
Oh may my whole deportment prove
    A copy, Lord, of thine.

26

Temperance

Take heed to yourselves, lest at any time your hearts be overcharged with surfeiting, and drunkenness, and cares of this life, and so that day come upon you unawares. *Luke xxi. 34.*

> The world employs its various snares,
> Of hopes and pleasures, pains and cares,
>   And chain'd to earth I lie:
> When shall my fetter'd powers be free,
> And leave these seats of vanity,
>   And upward learn to fly?

27

Gravity and Sincerity

In all things showing thyself a pattern of good works: in doctrine showing uncorruptness, gravity, sincerity.

Titus ii. 7.

> Pure may I be, averse to sin,
>   Just, holy, merciful, and true;
> And let thine image form'd within,
>   Shine out in all I speak or do.

28

Watchfulness

Blessed are those servants, whom the Lord when he cometh shall find watching: verily I say unto you, that he shall gird himself, and make them to sit down to meat, and will come forth and serve them. *Luke xii.* 37.

Arm me with jealous care,
As in thy sight to live:
And oh, thy servant, Lord, prepare,
A strict account to give.

Help me to watch and pray,
And on thyself rely;
Assured if I my trust betray,
I shall for ever die.

29

Diligence in Worldly Calling

Study to be quiet, and to do your own business, and to work with your own hands, as we commanded you.
1 Thess. iv. 11.

Midst hourly cares, may love present
Its incense to thy throne;
And while the world our hands employs,
Our hearts be thine alone.

30

Eminent Holiness
the Desire of the Believer

Not as though I had already attained, either were already perfect: but I follow after, if that I may apprehend that for which also I am apprehended of Jesus Christ. *Phil. iii. 12.*

Oh for a closer walk with God,
  A calm and heavenly frame,
A light to shine upon the road
  That leads me to the Lamb!

Duties of the Believer—
In the Church

I

To Show Forth the Praises of God

Ye are a chosen generation, a royal priesthood, an holy nation, a peculiar people; that ye should show forth the praises of him who hath called you out of darkness into his marvellous light. *1 Pet. ii. 9.*

Not by your words alone,
  But by your actions show
How much from him you have received,
  How much to him you owe.

2

To Depart from All Iniquity

Let every one that nameth the name of Christ depart from iniquity. 2 *Tim. ii. 19.*

> Faith must obey her Father's will,
>   As well as trust his grace;
> A pardoning God is jealous still
>   For his own holiness.

3

Stedfastness in the Faith

Stand fast in the liberty wherewith Christ hath made us free, and be not entangled again with the yoke of bondage. *Gal. v. 1.*

> From Egypt lately freed
>   By the Redeemer's grace,
> A rough and thorny path we tread
>   In hopes to see his face.
>
> The flesh dislikes the way,
>   But faith approves it well;
> This only leads to endless day,
>   All others lead to hell.

4

Zeal in Defence of the Gospel

I exhort you that ye should earnestly contend for the faith which was once delivered unto the saints. *Jude 3*.

In the conquests of thy might,
May I loyally delight;
In thy ever-spreading reign,
Triumph as my greatest gain:
Make me conscious by this sign,
Gracious Saviour, I am thine.

5

Zeal for Good Works

Let us consider one another to provoke unto love and to good works. *Heb. x. 24*.

Awake, my soul, awake, my love,
    And serve my Saviour here below,
In works which all the saints above
    And holy angels cannot do.

6

Zeal for Divine Worship

Not forsaking the assembling of ourselves together, as the manner of some is; but exhorting one another: and so much the more, as ye see the day approaching.

Heb. x. 25.

Oh let me always find a place,
Within the temples of thy grace;
Till God command my last remove,
To dwell in temples made above!

7

Concern for the Peace of the Church

Be perfect, be of good comfort, be of one mind, live in peace; and the God of love and peace shall be with you.

2 Cor. xiii. 11.

Make us of one heart and mind,
Courteous, pitiful, and kind;
Lowly, meek in thought and word,
Altogether like our Lord.

8

Concern for the Prosperity of the Church

Peace be within thy walls and prosperity within thy palaces. *Psa. cxxii.* 7.

> For our dear brethren's sake,
> Zion, we wish thee peace;
> Prosper, oh! prosper long,
> And may thy sons increase:
> We seek thy good, we love the road
> Which leads us to God's bless'd abode.

9

Mutual Love

Walk in love, as Christ also hath loved us, and hath given himself for us an offering and a sacrifice to God for a sweet-smelling savour. *Eph. v.* 2.

> Among the saints on earth
> Let mutual love be found;
> Heirs of the same inheritance,
> With mutual blessings crown'd.

10

Mutual Subjection

All of you be subject one to another, and be clothed
with humility: for God resisteth the proud, and giveth
grace to the humble. *1 Peter v. 5.*

> Lord, for ever at thy side
> May my place and portion be;
> Strip me of the robe of pride;
> Clothe me with humility.

11

Mutual Honour

Let nothing be done through strife or vainglory; but in
lowliness of mind let each esteem other better than
themselves. *Phil. ii. 3.*

> Oh let each esteem his brother
>   Better than himself to be;
> And let each prefer another,
>   Full of love, from envy free:
>   Happy are we,
>   When in this we all agree.

12

Mutual Forbearance

Forbearing one another, and forgiving one another, if any man have a quarrel against any: even as Christ forgave you, so also do ye. *Col. iii. 13.*

> May we each with each agree,
>   Through thy uniting grace:
> Our gift shall thine accepted be,
>   Our life be love and praise.

13

Mutual Candour

Judge not, that ye be not judged. Why beholdest thou the mote that is in thy brother's eye, but considerest not the beam that is in thine own eye? *Matt. vii. 1, 3.*

> Make us by thy transforming grace,
>   Great Saviour, daily more like thee:
> Thy fair example may we trace,
>   To teach us what we ought to be.

14
Mutual Forgiveness

Be ye kind one to another, tenderhearted, forgiving one another, even as God for Christ's sake hath forgiven you. *Eph. iv. 32.*

> "Is Christ divided?" What can part
>   The members from the Head?
> Oh how should those be one in heart
>   For whom our Saviour bled?

15
Mutual Admonition

I myself am persuaded of you, my brethren, that ye also are full of goodness, filled with all knowledge, able also to admonish one another. *Rom. xv. 14.*

> Bonds of everlasting love
>   Draw our souls in union,
> To our Father's house above,
>   To the saints' communion.
> Thither may our hopes ascend,
> There may all our labours end.

16

Mutual Consolation and Edification

Comfort yourselves together, and edify one another, even as also ye do. *1 Thess. v. 11.*

While we journey, let us
    Help each other on the road;
Foes on every side beset us,
    Snares through all the way are strew'd:
        It behoves us,
        Each to bear a brother's load.

17

Mutual Intercession

Pray one for another.—The effectual fervent prayer of a righteous man availeth much. *James v. 16.*

Before our Father's throne
    We pour our ardent prayers;
Our fears, our hopes, our aims are one—
    Our comforts and our cares.

18

Unity of Sentiment

Whereto we have already attained, let us walk by the same rule, let us mind the same thing. *Phil. iii. 16.*

> Bound to one Lord, by common vow
>> In one great enterprize;
> One faith, one hope, one centre now,
>> Our common home, the skies.

19

Unity of Judgment

I beseech you, brethren, by the name of our Lord Jesus Christ, that ye all speak the same thing, and that there be no divisions among you; but that ye be perfectly joined together in the same mind and in the same judgment. *1 Cor. i. 10.*

> Lord, subdue our selfish will,
>> Each to each our tempers suit,
> By thy modulating skill,
>> Heart to heart, as lute to lute.

20

United Prayer

Where two or three are gathered together in my name, there am I in the midst of them. *Matt. xviii.* 20.

> Where two or three with sweet accord,
> Obedient to their sovereign Lord,
> Meet to recount his acts of grace,
> And offer solemn prayer and praise;
> There, saith the Saviour, will I be
> Amid the little company.

21

United Praise

Teaching and admonishing one another in psalms and hymns and spiritual songs, singing with grace in your hearts to the Lord. *Col. iii.* 16.

> Teach us, though in a world of sin,
> Heaven's bless'd employment to begin,
> To sing our great Redeemer's praise;
> And love his name, and learn his ways.

22

Pious Conversation

Let no corrupt communication proceed out of your mouth, but that which is good to the use of edifying, that it may minister grace unto the hearers. *Eph. iv. 29.*

Wheresoever two or three
Meet, a Christian company,
Grant us, Lord, to meet with thee:
  Gracious Saviour, hear!
When with friends beloved we stray,
Talking down the closing day,
Saviour, meet us in the way:
  Gracious Saviour, hear!

23

Compassion for the Weak

We that are strong ought to bear the infirmities of the weak, and not to please ourselves. *Rom. xv. 1.*

When weaker Christians we despise,
  We do the great Redeemer wrong;
For God, the gracious and the wise,
  Receives the feeble with the strong.

24

Compassion for the Afflicted

Remember them that are in bonds, as bound with them; and them which suffer adversity, as being yourselves also in the body. *Heb. xiii. 3.*

> With pity let my breast o'erflow,
> When I behold another's woe;
> And bear a sympathizing part,
> Whene'er I meet a wounded heart.

25

Compassion for the Poor

As we have therefore opportunity, let us do good unto all men, especially unto them who are of the household of faith. *Gal. vi. 10.*

> Awake, my charity, and feed
>   The hungry soul, and clothe the poor;
> In heaven are found no sons of need,
>   There all these duties are no more.

26

Compassion to Those Who Have Erred

Brethren, if a man be overtaken in a fault, ye which are spiritual, restore such an one in the spirit of meekness; considering thyself, lest thou also be tempted.

Gal. vi. 1.

Lord, we would strive, and hope, and wait,
The offending still to reinstate;
And when a broken heart we view,
Our Christian friendship quick renew.

27

Freedom from Slander

Speak not evil one of another, brethren. He that speaketh evil of his brother, and judgeth his brother, speaketh evil of the law, and judgeth the law: but if thou judge the law, thou art not a doer of the law, but a judge. *James iv. 11.*

Love is a pure and heavenly flame,
And much regards a brother's name;
It hopeth all things, and believes,
Nor easily a charge receives.

28

Esteem for the Ministry

We beseech you to know them which labour among you, and are over you in the Lord, and admonish you; and to esteem them very highly in love for their work's sake. *1 Thess. v. 12, 13.*

> How beauteous are their feet,
>   Who stand on Zion's hill;
> Who bring salvation on their tongues,
>   And words of peace reveal!

29

Prayer for the Ministry

Praying always with all prayer and supplication in the Spirit;—and for me, that utterance may be given unto me, that I may open my mouth boldly, to make known the mystery of the gospel. *Eph. vi. 18, 19.*

> With heavenly power, O Lord, defend
> Those whom we now to thee commend;
> Thy faithful messengers secure,
> And make them to the end endure.

30

Unbelief Should Be Guarded Against

Take heed, brethren, lest there be in any of you an evil
heart of unbelief, in departing from the living God.

Heb. iii. 12.

How oft, deceived by self and pride,
Has my weak heart been turn'd aside;
And, Jonah-like, has fled from thee,
Till thou hast look'd again on me!

31

Caution Against Apostasy

Looking diligently lest any man fail of the grace of
God; lest any root of bitterness springing up trouble
you, and thereby many be defiled. *Heb. xii. 15.*

What bright exchange, what treasure shall
be given,
For the lost birthright of a hope in heaven?
If lost the gem which empires could not buy,
What yet remains?—a dark eternity.

Duties of the Believer—In the World

I

Believers Are the Salt of the Earth

Ye are the salt of the earth: but if the salt have lost his savour, wherewith shall it be salted? it is thenceforth good for nothing, but to be cast out, and to be trodden under foot of men. *Matt. v. 13.*

> Strive thou with studious care to find
>   Some good thy hands may do;
> Some way to serve and bless mankind,
> Console the heart, relieve the mind,
>   And open comforts new.

2
Believers Are the Light of the World

Ye are the light of the world. *Matt. v. 14.*

Walk in the light—and thine shall be
    A path, though stormy, bright;
For God in love shall dwell with thee—
    And God himself is light!

3
The Universal Rule of Equity

All things whatsoever ye would that men should do to you, do ye even so to them: for this is the law and the prophets. *Matt. vii. 12.*

Blessed Redeemer, how divine,
How righteous is this rule of thine,
To do to all men just the same
As we expect or wish from them.

How bless'd would every nation prove
Thus ruled by equity and love!
All would be friends without a foe,
And form a paradise below.

4

To Glorify God by Holy Conduct

I beseech you as strangers and pilgrims, abstain from fleshly lusts, which war against the soul; having your conversation honest among the Gentiles. *1 Pet. ii. 11*.

Help thy servant to maintain
A profession free from stain;
That my sole reproach may be,
Following Christ, and fearing thee.

5

Abounding in the Work of the Lord

My beloved brethren, be ye stedfast, unmoveable, always abounding in the work of the Lord, forasmuch as ye know that your labour is not in vain in the Lord.
1 Cor. xv. 58.

Sow in the morn thy seed,
At eve hold not thy hand,
To doubt and fear give thou no heed,
Broad-cast it round thy land.

6

Decision of Character

No man can serve two masters: for either he will hate the one, and love the other; or else he will hold to the one, and despise the other. Ye cannot serve God and mammon. *Matt. vi. 24.*

Not a broken, brief obedience
Does the Lord of heaven demand;
He requires our whole allegiance,
Words and deeds, and heart and hand:
    God will hold divided sway
    With no deity of clay.

7

Holy Example

Let your light so shine before men, that they may see your good works, and glorify your Father which is in heaven. *Matt. v. 16.*

So let our lips and lives express
The holy gospel we profess;
So let our works and virtues shine
To prove the doctrine all divine.

8

Live in Peace with All Men

If it be possible, as much as lieth in you, live peaceably
with all men. *Rom. xii. 18.*

His purpose is that we should bear
    His image now on earth,
And by our peaceful lives declare
    Our new and heavenly birth.

9

Love to Our Neighbour

If ye fulfil the royal law according to the scripture,
Thou shalt love thy neighbour as thyself, ye do well.

James ii. 8.

Love lays its own advantage by
    To seek its neighbour's good;
So God's own Son came down to die,
    And bought our lives with blood.

Love is the grace that keeps its power
    In all the realms above;
There faith and hope are known no more
    But saints for ever love.

10

Seek the Edification
of Our Neighbour

Let every one of us please his neighbour for his good to edification. *Rom. xv. 2.*

> May I from every act abstain,
> That hurts or gives another pain:
> Still may I feel my heart inclin'd
> To be the friend of all mankind.

11

Love to All Men

The Lord make you to increase and abound in love one toward another, and toward all men, even as we do toward you. *1 Thess. iii. 12.*

> May love, that shining grace,
> O'er all my powers preside;
> Direct my thoughts, suggest my words,
> And every action guide.

12

To Seek the Salvation of Others

He which converteth the sinner from the error of his way shall save a soul from death, and shall hide a multitude of sins. *James v. 20.*

> My God, I feel the mournful scene;
> My bowels yearn o'er dying men;
> And fain my pity would reclaim,
> And snatch the firebrands from the flame.

13

Give Due Honour to All

Render to all their dues: tribute to whom tribute is due; custom to whom custom; fear to whom fear; honour to whom honour. *Rom. xiii. 7.*

> Our sovereign with thy favour bless;
> Stablish the throne in righteousness,
>   Let wisdom hold the helm:
> The counsels of our senate guide,
> Let justice in our courts preside,
>   Rule thou, and bless the realm.

14

Consistency

That ye may be blameless and harmless, the sons of God, without rebuke, in the midst of a crooked and perverse nation, among whom ye shine as lights in the world. *Phil. ii. 15.*

That wisdom, Lord, on us bestow
  From every evil to depart,
To stop the mouth of every foe,
  While upright both in life and heart,
The proof of godly fear we give,
And show them how the Christians live.

15

Circumspection

See then that ye walk circumspectly, not as fools, but as wise. Redeeming the time, because the days are evil.
Eph. v. 15, 16.

Let every flying hour confess
I gain the gospel fresh renown;
And when my life and labours cease,
May I possess the promised crown.

16

Discretion

A good man sheweth favour, and lendeth: he will guide his affairs with discretion. *Psalm cxii. 5.*

> Believers love what God commands,
>   And in his ways delight;
> Their gracious words, and holy hands
>   Show that their faith is right.
>
> Their converse is with God above,
>   Their labours bless mankind;
> Their works of mercy, peace, and love,
>   Through Christ acceptance find.

17

Moderation

Let your moderation be known unto all men. The Lord is at hand. *Phil. iv. 5.*

> We'll look on all the toys below
> With such disdain as angels do;
> And wait the call that bids us rise
> To mansions promised in the skies.

18

Forbearance

Dearly beloved, avenge not yourselves, but rather give place unto wrath: for it is written, Vengeance is mine; I will repay, saith the Lord. *Rom. xii. 19.*

> May I feel beneath my wrongs
> Vengeance to the Lord belongs;
> Nor a worse requital dare,
> Than the meek revenge of prayer:
> Much forgiven, may I learn,
> Love for hatred to return.

19

Industry

Let a man labour, working with his hands the thing which is good, that he may have to give to him that needeth. *Eph. iv. 28.*

> To thee my very life I owe;
> From thee do all my comforts flow;
> And every blessing which I need
> Must from thy bounteous hand proceed.

20

Integrity

That ye may walk honestly toward them that are without, and that ye may have lack of nothing. *1 Thess. iv. 12.*

Come, let us search our ways, and try
　　Have they been just and right;
Is the great rule of equity
　　Our practice and delight?

In all we sell, in all we buy,
　　Is justice our design?
Do we remember God is nigh,
　　And fear the wrath Divine?

21

Fidelity

He that is faithful in that which is least is faithful also in much: and he that is unjust in the least is unjust also in much. *Luke xvi. 10.*

Thy gifts are only then enjoy'd
　　When used as talents lent;
Those talents only well employ'd
　　When in his service spent.

22

Truth and Sincerity

Wherefore, putting away lying, speak every man truth with his neighbour: for we are members one of another. *Eph. iv. 25.*

Let those who bear the Christian name
    Their holy vows fulfil;
The saints, the followers of the Lamb,
    Are men of honour still.

23

Gentleness and Meekness

Speak evil of no man, to be no brawlers, but gentle, showing all meekness to all men. *Tit. iii. 2.*

Bless'd are the men of peaceful life,
Who quench the coals of growing strife,
They shall be called the heirs of bliss,
The sons of God, the sons of peace.

24

Benevolence

Pure religion and undefiled before God and the Father is this, To visit the fatherless and widows in their affliction, and to keep himself unspotted from the world. *James i. 27.*

> The poor are always with us here:
>   'Tis our great Father's plan,
> That mutual wants and mutual care
>   Should bind us man to man.

25

Overcome Evil with Good

If thine enemy hunger feed him: if he thirst, give him drink: for in so doing thou shalt heap coals of fire on his head. Be not overcome of evil, but overcome evil with good. *Rom. xii. 20, 21.*

> Thus artists melt the sullen ore of lead,
> With heaping coals of fire upon its head;
> In the kind warmth the metal learns to glow,
> And loose from dross the silver runs below.

26

Perseverance in Doing Good

Let us not be weary in well doing: for in due season we shall reap if we faint not. *Gal. vi. 9.*

> Meek pilgrim Zionward, if thou
> Hast put thy hand unto the plough,
> Oh look not back, nor droop dismay'd,
> At thought of victory delay'd:
> Doubt not that thou, in season due,
> Shall own his gracious promise true;
> And thou shalt share their glorious lot,
> Whom doing well hath wearied not.

27

Submission to Authority

Put them in mind to be subject to principalities and powers, to obey magistrates, to be ready to every good work. *Titus iii. 1.*

> Lord, thou hast bid thy people pray
> For all that bear the sovereign sway,
>   Who as thy servants reign;
> Rulers, and governors, and powers—
> Behold, in faith we pray for ours;
>   Nor let us plead in vain.

28

Universal Holiness the Believer's Aim

Whatsoever things are true, whatsoever things are honest, whatsoever things are just, whatsoever things are pure, whatsoever things are lovely, whatsoever things are of good report; if there be any virtue, and if there be any praise, think on these things. *Phil. iv. 8.*

Father of eternal grace,
Glorify thyself in me;
Meekly beaming in my face,
May the world thine image see.

29

Believer's Humble Confession

So likewise ye, when ye shall have done all those things which are commanded you, say, We are unprofitable servants: we have done that which was our duty to do.
Luke xvii. 10.

My present triumphs, and my past,
Are thine, and must be to the last;
And if the crown of life I wear,
Thy hand alone must place it there.

30

The Great Motive to All Duty

Ye are not your own; for ye are bought with a price:
therefore glorify God in your body, and in your spirit,
which are God's. *1 Cor. vi. 19, 20.*

> Oh! grant us, Lord, to feel and own
>   The power of love divine;
> The blood which doth for sin atone,
>   The grace which makes us thine.

Joys of
the Believer

I

Joy in God

Let all those that put their trust in thee rejoice: let
them ever shout for joy, because thou defendest them:
let them also that love thy name be joyful in thee.

Psalm v. 11.

When with his smiles my soul he deigns to
    bless,
  Nor cares nor crosses can my peace destroy,
Possessing all things if I him possess,
  Enjoying all things if I him enjoy.

2

Joy in Christ

We are the circumcision, which worship God in the
spirit, and rejoice in Christ Jesus, and have no confidence in the flesh. *Phil. iii. 3.*

The opening heavens around me shine
    With beams of sacred bliss,
While Jesus shows his heart is mine,
    And whispers, I am his.

3

Joy in the Holy Ghost

The kingdom of God is not meat and drink; but
righteousness, and peace, and joy in the Holy Ghost.

Rom. xiv. 17.

Holy Ghost, dispel our sadness,
    Pierce the cloud of sinful night;
Come, thou source of joy and gladness,
    Breathe thy life, and shed thy light.

4

The Gospel a Source of Joy

Blessed is the people that know the joyful sound: they shall walk, O Lord, in the light of thy countenance.

Psalm lxxxix. 15.

Bless'd are the souls that hear and know
    The gospel's joyful sound;
Peace shall attend the path they go,
    And light their steps surround.

5

The Atonement a Source of Joy

We joy in God through our Lord Jesus Christ, by whom we have now received the atonement. *Rom. v. 11.*

There is a fountain fill'd with blood,
    Drawn from Immanuel's veins,
And sinners plunged beneath that flood
    Lose all their guilty strains.

The dying thief rejoic'd to see
    That fountain in his day;
And here may I, though vile as he,
    Wash all my sins away.

6

The Scriptures a Source of Joy

Thy words were found, and I did eat them; and thy word was unto me the joy and rejoicing of mine heart: for I am called by thy name, O Lord God of hosts. *Jer. xv. 16.*

Oh may these heavenly pages be
    My ever dear delight;
And still new beauties may I see,
    And still increasing light.

7

The Sabbath a Source of Joy

This is the day which the Lord hath made; we will rejoice and be glad in it. *Psalm cxviii. 24.*

Oft as this peaceful day shall come,
    Lord, raise my thoughts from earthly
      things,
And bear them to my heavenly home,
    On faith and hope's celestial wings:
Till the last gleam of life decay,
In one eternal sabbath day.

8

Faith a Source of Joy

Whom having not seen, ye love; in whom, though now ye see him not, yet believing, ye rejoice with joy unspeakable and full of glory. *1 Pet. i. 8.*

A bleeding Saviour, seen by faith,
　　A sense of pardoning love,
A hope that triumphs over death,
　　Give joys like those above.

9

Pardon a Source of Joy

Blessed is he whose transgression is forgiven, whose sin is covered. Blessed is the man unto whom the Lord imputeth not iniquity, and in whose spirit there is no guile. *Psalm xxxii. 1, 2.*

The Saviour smiles! o'er my bless'd soul
New tides of hope tumultuous roll;
Earth has a joy unknown in heaven,
The new-born peace of sin forgiven;
Tears of such pure and deep delight,
Ye angels! never dimm'd your sight.

10

Hope of Glory a Source of Joy

By whom [Jesus Christ] we have access by faith into this grace wherein we stand, and rejoice in hope of the glory of God. *Rom. v. 2.*

> By faith to Pisgah's top I fly,
>   And there delighted stand,
> To view beneath a cloudless sky,
>   The spacious promised land.
>
> The Lord of all the vast domain
>   Has promised it to me;
> The length and breadth of all the plain,
>   As far as faith can see.

11

Godly Fear a Source of Joy

Blessed is every one that feareth the Lord; that walketh in his ways. For thou shalt eat the labour of thine hands: happy shalt thou be, and it shall be well with thee. *Psalm cxxviii. 1, 2.*

> Happy, beyond description, he
>   Who fears the Lord his God;
> Who hears his threats with holy awe,
>   And trembles at his rod.

12

Obedience a Source of Joy

I will delight myself in thy commandments which I
have loved. *Psalm cxix.* 47.

Then shall my heart have inward joy,
    And keep my face from shame,
When all thy statutes I obey,
    And honour all thy name.

13

Communion with God a Source of Joy

There be many that say, Who will show us any good?
Lord, lift thou up the light of thy countenance upon
us. Thou hast put gladness in my heart, more than in
the time that their corn and their wine increased.

Psalm iv. 6, 7.

Lord, what is life? if spent with thee,
    In humble praise and prayer,
How long or short my life may be
    I feel no anxious care:
Though life depart, my joys shall last,
When life and all its joys are past.

14

Communion of Saints a Source of Joy

My goodness extendeth not to thee; but to the saints
that are in the earth, and to the excellent, in whom is
all my delight. *Psalm xvi. 2, 3.*

> If 'tis sweet to mingle where
> Christians meet for fervent prayer;
> If 'tis sweet with them to raise
> Songs of holy joy and praise;
> Passing sweet that state must be,
> Where they meet eternally.

15

Prayer a Source of Joy

Even them will I bring to my holy mountain, and
make them joyful in my house of prayer. *Isaiah lvi. 7.*

> Prayer makes the darken'd cloud withdraw,
> Prayer climbs the ladder Jacob saw;
> Gives exercise to faith and love,
> Brings every blessing from above.

16

Salvation a Source of Joy

We will rejoice in thy salvation, and in the name of our God we will set up our banners. *Psalm xx. 5.*

Salvation! oh the joyful sound!
   'Tis pleasure to our ears;
A sovereign balm for every wound,
   A cordial for our fears.

17

Early Piety a Source of Joy

O satisfy us early with thy mercy; that we may rejoice and be glad all our days. *Psalm xc. 14.*

Grace is a plant, where'er it grows,
   Of pure and heavenly root;
But fairest in the young it shows,
   And yields the sweetest fruit.

18

A Good Conscience a Source of Joy

Our rejoicing is this, the testimony of our conscience, that in simplicity and godly sincerity, not with fleshly wisdom, but by the grace of God, we have had our conversation in the world. *2 Cor. i. 12.*

O happy soul, that lives on high,
  While men lie grovelling here;
Whose hopes are fix'd above the sky,
  And faith forbids his fear.

His conscience cleans'd from all his sins,
  Love, peace, and joy combine
To form a life whose holy springs
  Are hidden and divine.

19

Benevolence a Source of Joy

Remember the words of the Lord Jesus, how he said, It is more blessed to give than to receive. *Acts xx. 35.*

Bless'd is the man whose heart expands
  At melting pity's call,
And the rich blessings of whose hands
  Like heavenly manna fall.

20

Tribulation a Source of Joy

We glory in tribulation: knowing that tribulation worketh patience; and patience, experience; and experience, hope. *Rom. v. 3, 4.*

Then let us wait the' appointed day,
　　Nor call this world our home;
To pilgrims in a foreign land,
　　Afflictions needs must come.

Who rules the world, o'errules their end,
　　They destined are for good;
And bear the saints to realms of rest,
　　Though mighty as a flood.

21

Temporal Blessings Sources of Joy

Ye shall eat in plenty, and be satisfied, and praise the name of the Lord your God, that hath dealt wondrously with you: and my people shall never be ashamed. *Joel ii. 26.*

Thy bounty gilds the path of life
　　With every cheering ray,
And oft restrains the rising tear,
　　Or wipes that tear away.

22

The Divine Blessing a Source of Joy

The blessing of the Lord, it maketh rich, and he addeth no sorrow with it. *Prov. x. 22.*

> Better than life itself thy love,
>   Dearer than all beside to me;
> For whom have I in heaven above,
>   Or what on earth, compared to thee?

23

The Divine Protection a Source of Joy

Because thou hast been my help, therefore in the shadow of thy wings will I rejoice. *Psalm lxiii. 7.*

> Since thou hast been my help,
>   To thee my spirit flies;
> And on thy watchful providence
>   My cheerful hope relies.

24

Divine Acceptance a Source of Joy

Go thy way, eat thy bread with joy, and drink thy wine
with a merry heart; for God now accepteth thy work.

Eccles. ix. 7.

Whilst I see thy love to me,
    Every object teems with joy;
Here, oh may I walk with thee,
    Then into thy presence die!
Let me but thyself possess,
Total sum of happiness;
Real bliss I then shall prove—
Heaven below, and heaven above.

25

Joy Following Sorrow

Weeping may endure for a night; but joy cometh in
the morning. *Psalm xxx.* 5.

When comforts are declining,
    He grants the soul again,
A season of clear shining,
    To cheer it after rain.

26

Joy the Duty of the Believer

Be glad in the Lord, and rejoice, ye righteous: and shout for joy, all ye that are upright in heart.

Psalm xxxii. 11.

Let those refuse to sing
    Who never knew the Lord;
But children of the heavenly King
    Should speak their joys abroad.

27

Joy to be Sought Through Christ

Hitherto have ye asked nothing in my name: ask, and ye shall receive, that your joy may be full. *John xvi. 24.*

Dark and cheerless is the morn,
    Unaccompanied by thee;
Joyless is the day's return,
    Till thy mercy's beams we see:
Day-spring from on high, be near;
Day-star, in our hearts appear.

28

Believer's Joy Is Satisfying

Blessed is the man whom thou choosest, and causest to approach unto thee, that he may dwell in thy courts: we shall be satisfied with the goodness of thy house, even of thy holy temple. *Psalm lxv. 4.*

> These are the joys which satisfy,
>   And sanctify the mind;
> Which make the spirit mount on high,
>   And leave the world behind.

29

Believer's Joy Is Abiding

These things have I spoken unto you, that my joy might remain in you, and that your joy might be full.
John xv. 11.

> Art thou not mine, my living Lord?
>   And can my hope, my comfort die,
> Fix'd on thine everlasting word—
>   The word that built the earth and sky.

30

Believer Has Joy in Death

Lord, now lettest thou thy servant depart in peace, according to thy word: for mine eyes have seen thy salvation. *Luke ii. 29, 30.*

> When we have number'd all our years,
>   And stand, at length, on Jordan's brink;
> Though the flesh fail with mortal fears,
>   Oh! let not then the spirit sink:
> But strong in faith, and hope, and love,
> Plunge through the stream to rise above.

31

Heaven the Consummation of Joy

Well done, thou good and faithful servant: thou hast been faithful over a few things, I will make thee ruler over many things: enter thou into the joy of thy Lord.
Matt. xxv. 21.

> Soldier of Christ, well done!
>   Praise be thy new employ;
> And while eternal ages run,
>   Rest in thy Saviour's joy.

AUGUST

Sorrows of
the Believer

I

Believer Forewarned of Sorrow

These things I have spoken unto you, that in me ye
might have peace. In the world ye shall have tribulation: but be of good cheer; I have overcome the world.

John xvi. 33.

The path of sorrow, and that path alone,
Leads to the land where sorrow is unknown.
No traveller e'er reached that bless'd abode,
Who found not thorns and briars in his road.

2

Sources of Sorrow— Loss of Divine Favour

Restore unto me the joy of thy salvation; and uphold me with thy free Spirit. *Psalm li. 12.*

> Ah! why, by passing clouds oppress'd,
> Should vexing thoughts distract thy breast?
> Turn, turn to Him, in every pain,
> Whom never suppliant sought in vain.

3

Sources of Sorrow—Indwelling Sin

I see another law in my members, warring against the law of my mind, and bringing me into captivity to the law of sin which is in my members. *Rom. vii. 23.*

> Nature may raise her fleshly strife,
> Reluctant to the heavenly life:
> But grace omnipotent at length
> Shall arm the saint with saving strength,
> Through the sharp war with aids attend,
> And his last conflict sweetly end.

4

Sources of Sorrow—A Deceitful Heart

The heart is deceitful above all things, and desperately wicked: who can know it? *Jer. xvii. 9.*

> With flowing tears, Lord, I confess,
> My folly and unstedfastness;
> When shall this heart more stable be,
> Fix'd by thy grace alone on thee?

5

Sources of Sorrow—
Ingratitude of the Ungodly

They that render evil for good are mine adversaries; because I follow the thing that good is. Forsake me not, O Lord: O my God, be not far from me.

Psalm xxxviii. 20, 21.

> If wounded love my bosom swell,
> Deceived by those I prized too well;
> He shall his pitying aid bestow,
> Who felt on earth severer woe:
> At once betray'd, denied, or fled,
> By those who shared his daily bread.

6

Sources of Sorrow—
Reproach of the World

Let us go forth therefore unto him without the camp, bearing his reproach. *Heb. xiii. 13.*

If on my face, for thy dear name,
   Shame and reproach shall be,
I'll hail reproach, and welcome shame,
   If thou remember me.

7

Sources of Sorrow—Persecution

Though I walk in the midst of trouble, thou wilt revive me: thou shalt stretch forth thine hand against the wrath of mine enemies, and thy right hand shall save me. *Ps. cxxxviii. 7.*

Man may trouble and distress me,
'Twill but drive me to thy breast;
Life with trials hard may press me,
Heaven will bring me sweeter rest.

8

Sources of Sorrow—
Earthly Losses and Bereavements

Naked came I out of my mother's womb, and naked
shall I return thither: the Lord gave and the Lord hath
taken away; blessed be the name of the Lord. *Job i. 21.*

> Oh! blessed be the hand that gave;
>   Still blessed when it takes:
> Blessed be he who smites to save,
>   Who heals the heart he breaks:
> Perfect and true are all his ways
> Whom heaven adores, and earth obeys.

9

Sources of Sorrow—The Sins of Others

Rivers of water run down mine eyes, because they keep
not thy law. *Psalm cxix. 136.*

> I sorrow for the mental night
>   In which mankind around me lie:
> Almighty Father, by thy might,
>   Arouse them from their lethargy.

10

Sources of Sorrow—
The Number of the Wicked

Broad is the way, that leadeth to destruction, and many there be which go in thereat: because strait is the gate, and narrow is the way, which leadeth unto life, and few there be that find it. *Matt. vii. 13, 14.*

> Strait is the way, the door is strait,
> Which lead to joys on high:
> 'Tis but a few that find the gate,
> While crowds mistake, and die.

11

Sorrow Chosen Rather than Sin

Moses, when he was come to years, refused to be called the son of Pharaoh's daughter; choosing rather to suffer affliction with the people of God, than to enjoy the pleasures of sin for a season. *Heb. xi. 24, 25.*

> It is not for me to be seeking my bliss,
> And building my hopes in a region like this
> I look for a city which hands have not piled;
> I pant for a country by sin undefiled.

12

Believer's Confidence in Trouble

Although the fig tree shall not blossom, neither shall fruit be in the vines; the labour of the olive shall fail, and the fields shall yield no meat; the flock shall be cut off from the fold, and there shall be no herd in the stalls: yet I will rejoice in the Lord, I will joy in the God of my salvation. *Hab. iii.* 17, 18.

> Although my wealth and comfort's lost,
>   My blooming hopes cut off I see,
> Yet will I in my Saviour trust,
>   Whose matchless grace can reach to me.

13

Believer's Comfort in Trouble

This is my comfort in my affliction: for thy word hath quickened me. *Psalm cxix, 50.*

> Thus trusting in thy word, I tread
>   The narrow path of duty on;
> What though some cherish'd joys are fled?
>   What though some flattering dreams are
>   gone?
> Yet purer brighter joys remain:
> Why should my spirit then complain?

14

Christ an Example to the Afflicted

Even hereunto were ye called: because Christ also suffered for us, leaving us an example, that ye should follow his steps. *1 Pet. ii. 21.*

> Our glorious Leader claims our praise
>   For his own pattern given,
>   While the long cloud of witnesses
>   Show the same path to heaven.

15

The Patriarchs Examples to the Afflicted

Wherefore seeing we also are compassed about with so great a cloud of witnesses, let us lay aside every weight, and the sin which doth so easily beset us, and let us run with patience the race that is set before us. *Heb. xii. 1.*

> Once they were mourning here below,
>   And wet their couch with tears;
> They wrestled hard, as we do now,
>   With sins, and doubts, and fears.

16

The Prophets Examples to the Afflicted

Take, my brethren, the prophets, who have spoken in the name of the Lord, for an example of suffering affliction, and of patience. *James v. 10.*

> And shall not we aspire,
> Like them our course to run?
> The crown if we would wear,
> The cross must first be borne.
> Divinely taught, they show'd the way,
> First to believe, and then obey.

17

Benefits of Affliction—Self-Abasement

Surely after that I was instructed, I smote upon my thigh: I was ashamed, yea, even confounded, because I did bear the reproach of my youth. *Jer. xxxi. 19.*

> Dumb at thy feet I lie,
> For thou hast brought me low;
> Remove thy judgments, lest I die;
> I faint beneath thy blow.

18

Benefits of Affliction—Contrition for Sin

I will go and return to my place, till they acknowledge their offence, and seek my face: in their affliction they will seek me early. *Hos. v. 15.*

What though afflictions pierced my heart!
I bless the hand that caused the smart;
It taught my tears awhile to flow,
But saved me from eternal woe.

19

Benefits of Affliction—Patience

The trying of your faith worketh patience. But let patience have her perfect work, that ye may be perfect and entire, wanting nothing. *James i. 3, 4.*

Through waves, and clouds, and storms,
    He gently clears thy way:
Wait thou his time—the darkest night
    Shall end in brightest day.

20

Benefits of Affliction—Humility

If I be wicked, woe unto me; and if I be righteous, yet
will I not lift up mine head. I am full of confusion;
therefore see thou mine affliction. *Job x. 15.*

To the heart truly humbled by woe,
The anointing of joy shall be given;
To the tears that from penitence flow,
The peace that's the' forerunner of heaven.

21

Benefits of Affliction—Submission

I was dumb, I opened not my mouth; because thou
didst it. *Psalm xxxix. 9.*

Take all, great God, I will not grieve,
But still will wish that I had still to give:
    I hear thy voice, thou bidd'st me quit
My paradise; I bless, and do submit;
    I will not murmur at thy word,
Nor beg thy angel to sheath up his sword.

22

Benefits of Affliction—Hope

Why art thou cast down, O my soul? and why art thou disquieted in me? hope thou in God: for I shall yet praise him for the help of his countenance. *Psalm xlii. 5.*

> The gloomiest day hath gleams of light,
>   The darkest wave hath bright foam near it;
> And twinkles through the cloudiest night
>   Some solitary star to cheer it.

23

Benefits of Affliction—Holiness

Now no chastening for the present seemeth to be joyous, but grievous: nevertheless, afterward it yieldeth the peaceable fruit of righteousness unto them which are exercised thereby. *Heb. xii. 11.*

> Our hearts are fasten'd to this world
>   By strong and endless ties;
> But every sorrow cuts a string,
>   And urges us to rise.

24

Benefits of Affliction—
Tries Our Sincerity

He knoweth the way that I take: when he hath tried me, I shall come forth as gold. *Job xxiii. 10.*

> Though sorrows rise, and dangers roll
> In waves of darkness o'er my soul;
> Though friends are false, and love decays,
> And few and evil are my days—
> Yet even in nature's utmost ill,
> I love thee, Lord! I love thee still.

25

Benefits of Affliction—
Brings Sin to Remembrance

If they be bound in fetters, and be holden in cords of affliction; then he showeth them their work, and their transgressions that they have exceeded. *Job xxxvi. 8, 9.*

> My former hopes are fled,
>   My terror now begins;
> I feel, alas! that I am dead
>   In trespasses and sins.

26

Benefits of Affliction—Leads to Prayer

O remember not against us former iniquities: let thy tender mercies speedily prevent us: for we are brought very low. *Psalm lxxix. 8.*

> Ah! whither could we flee for aid
> When tempted, desolate, dismay'd;
> Or how the hosts of hell defeat,
> Had suffering saints no mercy-seat?

27

Benefits of Affliction—
Brings Us Back to God

I will hedge up thy way with thorns, and make a wall, that she shall not find her paths.—Then shall she say, I will go and return to my first husband; for then was it better with me than now. *Hos. ii. 6, 7.*

> Long unafflicted, undismay'd,
> In pleasure's path secure I stray'd:
> Thou madest me feel thy chastening rod,
> And straight I turned unto my God.

28

Benefits of Affliction—
Exercises Our Faith

Ye are in heaviness through manifold temptations:
that the trial of your faith, being much more precious
than of gold that perisheth, though it be tried with
fire, might be found unto praise and honour and glory
at the appearing of Jesus Christ. *1 Pet. i. 6, 7.*

Dark are the ways of Providence,
    While those who love thee groan;
Thy reasons lie conceal'd from sense,
    Mysterious and unknown.

29

Benefits of Affliction—
Teaches Our Frailty

Mine age is departed, and is removed from me as a
shepherd's tent: I have cut off like a weaver my life: he
will cut me off with pining sickness. *Isa. xxxviii. 12.*

Lord, let me know mine end,
    My days, how brief their date,
That I may timely comprehend
    How frail my best estate.

30

Benefits of Affliction—
Remind Us of Former Mercies

We had the sentence of death in ourselves, that we should not trust in ourselves, but in God which raiseth the dead: who delivered us from so great a death, and doth deliver: in whom we trust that he will yet deliver us. *2 Cor. i. 9, 10.*

His love in times past forbids me to think
He'll leave me at last in trouble to sink:
Each sweet Ebenezer I have in review
Confirms his good pleasure to help me quite through.

31

Affliction Succeeded by Glory

Our light affliction, which is but for a moment, worketh for us a far more exceeding and eternal weight of glory. *2 Cor. iv. 17.*

All trials and sorrows the Christian prepare
For the rest that remaineth above;
On earth tribulation awaits him, but there
The smile of unchangeable love.

SEPTEMBER

Temptations of the Believer

I

Temptations Permitted by God

The Lord said unto Satan, Behold, all that he hath is in thy power; only upon himself put not forth thine hand. *Job i. 12.*

Still thine integrity hold fast,
     The tempter's counsel spurn,
Hope against hope, and God at last,
     Will for thy help return.

2

God Does Not Tempt to Sin

Let no man say when he is tempted, I am tempted of God: for God cannot be tempted with evil, neither tempteth he any man: but every man is tempted, when he is drawn away of his own lust, and enticed.

James i. 13, 14.

My crimes, though great, do not surpass
The power and glory of thy grace;
Oh! wash my soul from every sin,
And make my guilty conscience clean.

3

Temptations—From Satan

Lest Satan should get an advantage of us: for we are not ignorant of his devices. *2 Cor. ii. 11.*

Fear not Satan's strong temptations
    Though they tease thee day by day,
And thy evil inclinations
    Overwhelm thee with dismay!
        Thou shalt conquer,
Through the Lamb's redeeming blood.

4

Temptations—From a Depraved Nature

I find then a law, that, when I would do good, evil is
present with me. *Rom. vii. 21.*

> Oh! who can free my troubled mind
>   From sin's oppressive load?
> O wretched man! how shall I find
>   Acceptance with my God.
>
> My soul with transport turns to thee,
>   To thee my Saviour turns;
> Cleansed by thy blood, and saved by grace,
>   My soul no longer mourns.

5

Temptations—From the Love of Riches

They that will be rich fall into temptation and a snare,
and into many foolish and hurtful lusts, which drown
men in destruction and perdition. *1 Tim. vi. 9.*

> Oh lay not up upon this earth
> Your hopes, your joys, your treasure,
> Here sorrow clouds the pilgrim's path,
>   And blights each opening pleasure.
> All, all below must fade and die,

The dearest hopes we cherish,
Scenes touch'd with brightest radiancy,
Are all decreed to perish.

6

Temptations—From the Fear of Man

The fear of man bringeth a snare: but whoso putteth
his trust in the Lord shall be safe. *Prov. xxix. 25.*

The taunts and frowns of men of earth,
What are they all to me!
Oh they are things of little worth,
Weigh'd with one smile from Thee,
Who bore a sorrow deeper far,
Than all these stingless trifles are.

7

Temptation to Neglect Good Works

Ye did run well; who did hinder you, that ye should
not obey the truth? *Gal. v. 7.*

Better that we had never known
The way to heaven through saving grace,
Than basely in our lives disown,
And slight and mock thee to thy face.

8

Temptation to Legal Dependance

Are ye so foolish? having begun in the Spirit, are ye now made perfect in the flesh? *Gal. iii. 3.*

Go, you that rest upon the law,
And toil and seek salvation there;
Look to the flame that Moses saw,
And shrink, and tremble, and despair.

But I'll retire beneath thy cross—
Saviour, at thy dear feet I'll lie;
And the keen sword that justice draws,
Flaming and red, shall pass me by.

9

Temptation to Formality in Religion

Be watchful, and strengthen the things which remain, that are ready to die: for I have not found thy works perfect before God. *Rev. iii. 2.*

God is a Spirit just and wise;
He sees our inmost mind:
In vain to heaven we raise our cries,
And leave our souls behind.

10

Temptation to Slothfulness in Religion

Nevertheless I have somewhat against thee, because thou hast left thy first love. Remember therefore from whence thou art fallen, and repent, and do the first works. *Rev. ii. 4, 5.*

I need the influence of thy grace
 To speed me in the way,
Lest I should loiter in my pace,
 Or turn my feet astray.

11

Temptation to Self-Indulgence

I keep under my body, and bring it into subjection: lest that by any means, when I have preached to others, I myself should be a castaway. *1 Cor. ix. 27.*

When thy statutes I forsake,
 When my graces dimly shine,
When my covenant I break,
 Jesus, then remember thine:
  Check my wanderings
 By a look of love divine.

12

Temptation to Trifle with Sin

Shall we continue in sin, that grace may abound? God forbid. How shall we, that are dead to sin, live any longer therein? *Rom. vi. 1.*

> Shall we go on to sin,
>   Because thy grace abounds?
> Or crucify the Lord again,
>   And open all his wounds?
>   We will be slaves no more,
>   Since Christ has made us free;
> Has nail'd our tyrants to his cross,
>   And bought our liberty.

13

Temptation to Spiritual Pride

For who maketh thee to differ from another? and what hast thou that thou didst not receive? now if thou didst receive it, why dost thou glory, as if thou hadst not received it? *1 Cor. iv. 7.*

> Oft have I turn'd my eyes within,
> And brought to mind some latent sin
> But pride, the vice I most detest,
> Still lurks securely in my breast.

14

Temptation to Envy the Wicked

As for me, my feet were almost gone; my steps had well nigh slipped. For I was envious at the foolish, when I saw the prosperity of the wicked. *Psalm lxxiii. 2, 3.*

Their feet are in a slippery place;
Their riches swift as shadows fly;
Their honours end in deep disgrace;
In mirth they live, in anguish die.

15

Temptation to Mistrust Providence

If God so clothe the grass of the field, which to-day is, and to-morrow is cast into the oven, shall he not much more clothe you, O ye of little faith? *Matt. vi. 30.*

I know not what may soon betide,
Or how my wants shall be supplied;
But Jesus knows, and will provide.

When creature comforts fade and die,
Worldlings may weep—but why should I?
Jesus still lives, and still is nigh.

16

Temptation to Despair

I sink in deep mire, where there is no standing: I am
come into deep waters, where the floods overflow me.
I am weary of my crying: my throat is dried: mine eyes
fail while I wait for my God. *Psalm lxix. 2, 3.*

> Prostrate before thy mercy-seat,
>   I cannot if I would despair;
> None ever perish'd at thy feet,
>   And I would lie for ever there.

17

Temptation Humbles the Believer

Lest I should be exalted above measure through the
abundance of the revelations, there was given to me a
thorn in the flesh, the messenger of Satan to buffet me,
lest I should be exalted above measure. *2 Cor. xii. 7.*

> What though a thorn my bosom bears,
> And varied are the wants and cares,
>   That mark my chequer'd way!
> My God hath said, in whom I live,
> "My grace is thine, and strength I give
>   According to thy day."

18

Temptation to Be Resisted

For we wrestle not against flesh and blood, but against principalities, against powers, against the rulers of the darkness of this world, against spiritual wickedness in high places. *Eph. vi. 12.*

> From strength to strength go on,
>   Wrestle, and fight, and pray;
> Tread all the powers of darkness down,
>   And win the well-fought day.

19

Temptation to Be Avoided

Enter not into the path of the wicked, and go not in the way of evil men. Avoid it, pass not by it, turn from it, and pass away. *Prov. iv. 14, 15.*

> A wicked world and wicked heart
>   With Satan are combined:
> Each acts a too successful part,
>   In harassing my mind.

> But fighting in my Saviour's strength,
>   Though mighty are my foes,
> I shall a conqueror be at length
>   O'er all that can oppose.

20

Temptation Avoided
by Watchfulness and Prayer

Watch and pray, that ye enter not into temptation.

Matt. xxvi. 41.

Go to dark Gethsemane,
Ye that feel the tempter's power,
Your Redeemer's conflict see,
Watch with him one bitter hour;
Turn not from his griefs away,
Learn of Jesus Christ to pray.

21

Temptation Overcome by Faith

Above all, taking the shield of faith, wherewith ye shall be able to quench all the fiery darts of the wicked.

Eph. vi. 16.

Let faith exert its conquering power,
Say in thy tempted, trembling hour,
"My God, my Father, save thy son!"
'Tis heard—and all thy fears are done.

22

Believer Armed Against Temptation

Take unto you the whole armour of God, that ye may be able to withstand in the evil day, and having done all, to stand. *Eph. vi. 13.*

> The Christian warrior—see him stand
> In the whole armour of his God;
> The Spirit's sword is in his hand,
> His feet are with the gospel shod.

23

Preservation from Temptation

Because thou hast kept the word of my patience, I also will keep thee from the hour of temptation. *Rev. iii. 10.*

> Thus preserved from Satan's wiles,
>   Safe from dangers, free from fears,
> May I live upon thy smiles,
>   Till the promised hour appears:
> When the sons of God shall prove
> All their Father's boundless love.

24

Preservation in Temptation

Blessed is the man that endureth temptation: for when he is tried, he shall receive the crown of life, which the Lord hath promised to them that love him. *James i. 12.*

When aught shall tempt my soul to stray
From heavenly wisdom's narrow way,
To shun the precept's holy light,
Or quit my hold on Jesu's might,
May He who felt temptation's power
Still guard me in that dangerous hour.

25

Deliverance from Temptation

The Lord knoweth how to deliver the godly out of temptations. *2 Pet. ii. 9.*

What though fierce and strong temptations
    Press around thee on the way,
And thy sinful inclinations
    Often cause thee great dismay!
        Look to Jesus,
    Thou through him shalt gain the day.

26

Christ the Strength of the Tempted

My grace is sufficient for thee: for my strength is made perfect in weakness. *2 Cor. xii. 9.*

Why should I fear the darkest hour,
Or tremble at the tempter's power!
Jesus vouchsafes to be my tower.

Though hot the fight, why quit the field?
Why must I either fear or yield,
Since Jesus is my mighty shield?

27

Christ's Sympathy with the Tempted

In that he himself hath suffered being tempted, he is able to succour them that are tempted. *Heb. ii. 18.*

Touch'd with a sympathy within,
    He knows our feeble frame;
He knows what sore temptations mean,
    For he has felt the same.

28

Christ's Intercession for the Tempted

The Lord said, Simon, Simon, behold, Satan hath desired to have you, that he may sift you as wheat: but I have prayed for thee, that thy faith fail not. *Luke xxii. 31, 32.*

> Though faint my prayers, and cold my love
> My stedfast hope shall not remove,
> While Jesus intercedes above.
>
> Against me earth and hell combine;
> But on my side is power Divine;
> Jesus is all, and he is mine.

29

The Lord's Prayer for the Tempted

Lead us not into temptation; but deliver us from evil.

Matt. vi. 13.

> Protect us in the dangerous hour,
> And from the wily tempter's power,
>   Lord, set our spirits free;
> And if temptation should assail,
> May mighty grace o'er all prevail,
>   And lead our hearts to thee.

30

Freedom from Temptation in Heaven

To him that overcometh, will I grant to sit with me in
my throne, even as I also overcame, and am set down
with my Father in his throne. *Rev. iii. 21.*

> Though temptations now attend thee,
> And thou tread'st the thorny road,
> His right hand shall still defend thee,
> Soon he'll bring thee home to God:
> Full deliverance
> Thou shalt have in heaven above.

OCTOBER

Retrospections of
the Believer

I

Duty of Retrospection

Thou shalt remember all the way which the Lord thy
God led thee these forty years in the wilderness, to
humble thee, and to prove thee, to know what was in
thine heart, whether thou wouldst keep his commandments. *Deut. viii. 2.*

> Thus far the Lord has led me on,
> And made his truth and mercy known;
> And while I tread this desert land,
> New mercies shall new songs demand.

2

Of the Divine Help

Then Samuel took a stone, and set it between Mizpeh and Shen, and called the name of it Ebenezer, saying, Hitherto hath the Lord helped us. *1 Sam. vii. 12.*

Here I raise my Ebenezer,
  Hither, by thy help, I'm come:
And I hope, by thy good pleasure,
  Safely to arrive at home.

3

Of the Divine Guidance

Who am I, O Lord God? and what is my house, that thou hast brought me hitherto? and this was yet a small thing in thy sight, O Lord God. *2 Sam. vii. 18, 19.*

Render'd safe by his protection,
  I shall pass the watery waste;
Trusting to his wise direction,
  I shall gain the port at last;
    And with wonder,
  Think on toils and dangers past.

4

Of the Divine Faithfulness

Thou hast dealt well with thy servant, O Lord, according unto thy word. *Psalm cxix. 65.*

Since first the maze of life I trod,
　　Hast thou not hedged about my way,
My worldly vain designs withstood,
　　And robb'd my passions of their prey?
Thrice happy loss, which makes me see
My happiness alone in thee!

5

Of the Divine Forbearance

It is of the Lord's mercies that we are not consumed, because his compassions fail not. They are new every morning: great is thy faithfulness. *Lam. iii. 22, 23.*

Lift up to God the voice of praise,
　　Whose goodness, passing thought,
Loads every minute as it flies
　　With benefits unsought.

6

Of the Divine Mercy

He hath not dealt with us after our sins; nor rewarded us according to our iniquities. *Psalm ciii. 10.*

> He hath with a piteous eye
> Look'd upon our misery:
> Let us, then, with gladsome mind,
> Praise the Lord, for he is kind:
> For his mercies shall endure,
> Ever faithful, ever sure.

7

Of the Divine Counsel and Instruction

I will bless the Lord, who hath given me counsel: my reins also instruct me in the night seasons. *Psalm xvi. 7.*

> Sure the Lord thus far has brought me,
>   By his watchful tender care;
> Sure, 'tis he himself has taught me
>   How to seek his face by prayer:
> After so much mercy past,
> Will he give me up at last?

8

Of Divine Promises Fulfilled

Ye know in all your hearts and in all your souls, that not one thing hath failed of all the good things which the Lord your God spake concerning you; all are come to pass unto you, and not one thing hath failed thereof.

Josh. xxiii. 14.

In all my ways thy hand I own,
  Thy ruling providence I see;
Assist me still my course to run,
  And still direct my paths to thee.

9

Of Unnumbered Blessings

Many, O Lord my God, are thy wonderful works which thou hast done, and thy thoughts which are to us-ward: they cannot be reckoned up in order unto thee: if I would declare and speak of them, they are more than can be numbered. *Psalm xl. 5.*

For mercies countless as the sand,
  Which daily I receive
From Jesus, my Redeemer's hand,
  My soul, what canst thou give?

10

Of Early Pious Instruction

Continue thou in the things which thou hast learned
and hast been assured of, knowing of whom thou hast
learned them. 2 *Tim. iii. 14.*

> Lord, hast thou made me know thy ways?
>   Conduct me in thy fear;
> And grant me such supplies of grace
>   That I may persevere.

11

Of His Natural State

You that were sometime alienated and enemies in your
mind by wicked works, yet now hath he reconciled.
Col. i. 21.

> Plunged in a gulf of dark despair,
>   We wretched sinners lay,
> Without one cheerful beam of hope,
>   Or spark of glimmering day.

12

Of the Sins of His Life

How many are mine iniquities and sins? make me to know my transgression and my sin. *Job xiii. 23.*

My past transgressions pain me;
    Lord, cleanse my heart within;
And evermore restrain me
    From all presumptuous sin.

So let my whole behaviour,
    Thoughts, words, and actions be,
O God, my strength and Saviour,
    Acceptable to thee.

13

Of Past Unprofitableness

For when ye were the servants of sin, ye were free from righteousness. What fruit had ye then in those things whereof ye are now ashamed? *Rom. vi. 20, 21.*

Lord, I confess my numerous faults,
    How great my guilt has been;
Foolish and vain were all my thoughts,
    And all my life was sin.

14

Of the Season of Conversion

Giving thanks unto the Father, which hath made us meet to be partakers of the inheritance of the saints in light: who hath delivered us from the power of darkness, and hath translated us into the kingdom of his dear Son. *Col. i. 12, 13.*

Since the dear hour that brought me to thy foot,
And cut up all my follies by the root,
I never trusted in an arm but thine,
Nor hoped but in thy righteousness
    Divine:—
Cast at thy glorious feet, mine only plea
Is what it was, dependance upon Thee.

15

Of Spiritual Deliverance

Great is thy mercy toward me: and thou hast delivered my soul from the lowest hell. *Psalm lxxxvi. 13.*

He pardon'd my transgressions,
    Bade all my sorrows cease;
And, in his rich compassions,
    Restored my soul to peace.

16

Of Spiritual Enjoyments

I sat down under his shadow with great delight, and his fruit was sweet to my taste. He brought me to the banqueting house, and his banner over me was love.

Sol. Song ii. 3, 4.

Kindly he brought me to the place
Where stands the banquet of his grace;
He saw me faint, and o'er my head
The banner of his love he spread.

17

Of Support in Affliction

Unless thy law had been my delight, I should then have perished in mine affliction. *Psalm cxix. 92.*

God of my life, how good, how wise
    Thy judgments to my soul have been!
They were but blessings in disguise,
    The painful remedies of sin.
How different now thy ways appear,
Most merciful, when most severe!

18

Of Answers to Prayer

I love the Lord, because he hath heard my voice and my supplications. Because he hath inclined his ear unto me, therefore will I call upon him as long as I live.

Psalm cxvi. 1, 2.

Did ever trouble yet befall,
And he refuse to hear thy call?
And has he not his promise pass'd,
That thou shalt overcome at last?

19

Of Deliverance from Adversity

I will be glad and rejoice in thy mercy: for thou hast considered my trouble; thou hast known my soul in adversities. *Psalm xxxi.* 7.

Oh, magnify the Lord with me;
　　Come, join his name to bless:
To him did I in trouble flee;
　　He saved me from distress:
Oh, let him then your refuge be,
　　Nor shall you fail success.

20

Of Deliverance from Danger

Thou drewest near in the day that I called upon thee:
thou saidst, Fear not. O Lord, thou hast pleaded the
causes of my soul; thou hast redeemed my life.

Lam. iii. 57, 58.

> Be all my added life employ'd
>   Thy image in my soul to see:
> Fill with thyself the mighty void;
>   Enlarge my heart to compass thee.

21

Of Deliverance from Death

O Lord, thou hast brought up my soul from the grave:
thou hast kept me alive, that I should not go down to
the pit. *Psalm xxx. 3.*

> Thy mercy chased the shades of death,
>   And snatch'd me from the grave;
> Oh may thy praise employ that breath
>   Which mercy deigns to save!

22

Of the Vanity of Human Life

And Jacob said unto Pharaoh, The days of the years of my pilgrimage are an hundred and thirty years: few and evil have the days of the years of my life been. *Gen. xlvii. 9.*

> This life's a dream, an empty show,
> But the bright world to which we go
> Hath joys substantial and sincere:
> When shall I wake, and find me there?

23

Of Departed Friends

I would not have you to be ignorant, brethren, concerning them which are asleep, that ye sorrow not, even as others which have no hope. For if we believe that Jesus died and rose again, even so them also which sleep in Jesus will God bring with him. *1 Thess. iv. 13, 14.*

> Though loved and lost, not ours the pang of
> those
> Whose earth-born grief no heavenly balsam
> knows:
> We would not call their spirits from their home
> Where sin assails them not, and sorrow can-
> not come.

24

Aged Believer's Retrospect

O God, thou hast taught me from my youth: and hitherto have I declared thy wondrous works. Now also
when I am old and grey-headed, O God, forsake me
not. *Psalm lxxi. 17, 18.*

> Still hath my life new wonders seen
>   Repeated every year:
> Behold, my days which yet remain
>   I trust them to thy care.

25

Retrospection Should Lead to Gratitude

What shall I render unto the Lord for all his benefits
toward me? I will take the cup of salvation, and call
upon the name of the Lord. *Psalm cxvi. 12, 13.*

> When all thy mercies, O my God,
>   My rising soul surveys,
> Transported with the view I'm lost
>   In wonder, love, and praise.

26

Retrospection Should Lead to Self-Examination

I have considered the days of old, the years of ancient times. I call to remembrance my song in the night: I commune with mine own heart: and my spirit made diligent search. *Psalm lxxvii. 5, 6.*

> Help me, O Lord, to try my heart,
>   To search with strictest care,
> And all my thoughts, and words, and ways,
>   With Scripture to compare.

27

Retrospection Should Lead to Self-Abasement

And Jacob said, I am not worthy of the least of all thy mercies, and of all the truth, which thou hast shewed unto thy servant. *Gen. xxxii. 10.*

> Unworthy, Lord, of all
>   Thy mercies though we be,
> Yet for the greatest we may call,
>   The greatest are most free.

28

Retrospection Should Lead to Repentance

Surely it is meet to be said unto God, I have borne chastisement, I will not offend any more: that which I see not teach thou me: if I have done iniquity, I will do no more. *Job xxxiv. 31, 32.*

In thought, in will, in word and deed,
What evils have I done,
Against the God of grace and love,
His Spirit and his Son?

29

Retrospection Should Lead to Amendment of Life

I thought on my ways, and turned my feet unto thy testimonies. I made haste, and delayed not to keep thy commandments. *Psalm cxix. 59, 60.*

Thou art my portion, O my God;
Soon as I know thy way,
My heart makes haste to obey thy word,
And suffers no delay.

30

Retrospection Should Lead to Confidence in God

Return unto thy rest, O my soul; for the Lord hath dealt bountifully with thee. For thou hast delivered my soul from death, mine eyes from tears, and my feet from falling. *Psalm cxvi.* 7, 8.

> For this, when future sorrows rise,
> To him will I direct my cries;
> For this, through all my future days,
> Adore his name, and sing his praise.

31

Retrospection Should Lead to Devotedness to God

Only fear the Lord, and serve him in truth with all your heart: for consider how great things he hath done for you. *1 Sam. xii.* 24.

> My God, my King, thy various praise
> Shall fill the remnant of my days;
> Thy grace employ my humble tongue
> Till death and glory raise the song.

> May every hour successive bear
> Some thankful tribute to thine ear;
> And by thy grace accepted be,
> As works of love perform'd for Thee.

NOVEMBER

Anticipations of the Believer

I

Believer's Confidence in God

My times are in thy hand: make thy face to shine upon thy servant: save me for thy mercies' sake.

Psalm xxxi. 15, 16.

"My times are in thy hand,"
  My God, I wish them there;
My life, my friends, my soul, I leave
  Entirely to thy care.

2

Of Future Support

Trust in the Lord, and do good; so shalt thou dwell in the land, and verily thou shalt be fed. *Psalm xxxvii. 3, 4.*

> The birds without barn or storehouse are fed;
> From them let us learn to trust for our bread:
> His saints what is fitting shall ne'er be denied,
> So long as 'tis written, The Lord will provide.

3

Of Deliverance from Trouble

Thou, which hast shewed me great and sore troubles, shalt quicken me again, and shalt bring me up again from the depths of the earth. *Psalm lxxi. 20.*

> From every piercing sorrow
>   That heaves our breast to-day,
> Or threatens us to-morrow,
>   Hope turns our eyes away;
> On wings of faith ascending,
>   We see the land of light,
> And feel our sorrows ending
>   In infinite delight.

4

Of Being Kept by Christ

I know whom I have believed, and am persuaded that
he is able to keep that which I have committed unto
him against that day. *2 Tim. i. 12.*

> Beneath his smiles my heart has liv'd,
>   And part of heaven possess'd;
> I thank him for the grace receiv'd,
>   And trust him for the rest.

5

Of the Completion of the Work of Grace

Being confident of this very thing, that he which hath
begun a good work in you will perform it until the day
of Jesus Christ. *Phil. i. 6.*

> He will complete the work begun,
>   He will his own defend;
> Will give me strength my course to run,
>   And love me to the end.

6

Of the Triumphs of the Gospel

His name shall endure for ever: his name shall be con-
tinued as long as the sun: and men shall be blessed in
him: all nations shall call him blessed. *Psalm lxxii. 17.*

Lord, let the thought of that bright day
Kindle our hopes, and warm our love;
Cheer us while here on earth we pray,
And crown our songs in heaven above.

7

Of the End of His Warfare

The time of my departure is at hand. I have fought a
good fight, I have finished my course, I have kept the
faith. *2 Tim. iv. 6, 7.*

Oh most delightful hour by man
Experienced here below,
The hour that terminates his span
Of conflict and of woe!

8

Of Victory Over Satan

The God of peace shall bruise Satan under your feet shortly. *Rom. xvi. 20.*

> Now let my soul arise,
> And tread the tempter down;
> My Captain leads me forth
> To conquest and a crown:
> A feeble saint shall win the day,
> Though death and hell obstruct the way.

9

Of Victory Over Sin

O wretched man that I am! who shall deliver me from the body of this death? I thank God, through Jesus Christ our Lord. *Rom. vii. 24, 25.*

> Now to the God of victory
> Immortal thanks be paid,
> Who makes us conquerors while we die,
> Through Christ our living Head.

10

Of Victory Over the Grave

God will redeem my soul from the power of the grave:
for he shall receive me. *Psalm xlix. 15.*

There, till the archangel's trumpet sound,
    Ages of silence I shall lie;
Then from my earthly cell rebound,
    Glorious in immortality.

11

Of the Certainty of Death

When a few years are come, then I shall go the way
whence I shall not return. *Job xvi. 22.*

Welcome, sweet hour of full discharge,
That sets my longing soul at large;
Unbinds my chains, breaks up my cell,
And gives me with my God to dwell.

12

Of Support in the Hour of Death

Yea, though I walk through the valley of the shadow of death, I will fear no evil: for thou art with me; thy rod and thy staff they comfort me. *Psalm xxiii. 4.*

When the vale of death appears,
  (Faint and cold this mortal clay,)
Kind Forerunner, soothe my fears,
  Light me through the darksome way:
    Break the shadows,
    Usher in eternal day.

13

Of the End of the World

The day of the Lord will come as a thief in the night; in the which the heavens shall pass away with a great noise, and the elements shall melt with fervent heat, the earth also and the works that are therein shall be burned up. *2 Pet. iii. 10.*

Lo! it comes—that day of wonder!
  Louder chorals shake the skies:
Hades' gates are burst asunder;
  See the new-clothed myriads rise!

14

Of a Joyful Resurrection

I know that my Redeemer liveth, and that he shall stand at the latter day upon the earth: and though after my skin worms destroy this body, yet in my flesh shall I see God. *Job xix. 25, 26.*

Though worms may waste this with'ring clay,
　　When flesh and spirit sever;
My soul shall see eternal day,
　　And dwell with God for ever.

15

Of the Coming of Christ to Judgment

Behold, he cometh with clouds; and every eye shall see him, and they also which pierced him: and all kindreds of the earth shall wail because of him. *Rev. i. 7.*

Great God! what do I see and hear!
　　The end of things created:
The Judge of mankind doth appear
　　In clouds of glory seated;
The trumpet sounds, the graves restore
The dead which they contain'd before:
　　Prepare, my soul, to meet him.

16

Of Meeting the Judge

We must all appear before the judgment seat of Christ;
that every one may receive the things done in his body,
according to that he hath done, whether it be good or
bad. *2 Cor. v. 10.*

> Oh! on that day, that wrathful day,
> When man to judgment wakes from clay,
> Lord, be the trembling sinner's stay,
> Though heaven and earth shall pass away.

17

Of Entire Acquittal

Who shall lay any thing to the charge of God's elect?
It is God that justifieth. Who is he that condemneth?
It is Christ that died; yea rather, that is risen again,
who is even at the right hand of God, who also maketh
intercession for us. *Rom. viii. 33, 34.*

> Fear not the drum's earth-rending sound,
>   Dread not the day of doom;
> For He that is to be thy Judge,
>   Thy Saviour is become.

18

Of Participation in the Judgment

Do ye not know that the saints shall judge the world?

1 Cor. vi. 2.

See the Judge, our nature wearing,
　　Cloth'd in majesty divine;
Ye who long for his appearing
　　Then shall say, "This God is mine:"
　　　Gracious Saviour,
　　Own us in that day of thine!

19

Of Being Presented Faultless

Unto him that is able to keep you from falling, and to present you faultless before the presence of his glory with exceeding joy. *Jude 24.*

What transport then shall fill my heart,
　　When thou my worthless name wilt own;
When I shall see thee as thou art,
　　And know as I myself am known!

20

Of an Incorruptible Body

So when this corruptible shall have put on incorruption, and this mortal shall have put on immortality, then shall be brought to pass the saying that is written, Death is swallowed up in victory. *1 Cor. xv. 54.*

> Where then thy triumph, Grave? and where
>   thy sting,
> O sullen Death? what terror dost thou bring?
> We burst thine iron band, and soar on high—
> Glory to Christ the Lord, who brings us
>   victory!

21

Of a Glorious Body

Who shall change our vile body, that it may be fashioned like unto his glorious body, according to the working whereby he is able even to subdue all things unto himself. *Phil. iii. 21.*

> My flesh shall slumber, in the ground
> Till the last trumpet's joyful sound;
> Then burst the chains, with sweet surprise,
> And in my Saviour's image rise.

22

Of Being with Christ

To me to live is Christ, and to die is gain. For I am in a strait betwixt two, having a desire to depart, and to be with Christ, which is far better. *Phil. i. 21, 23.*

'Tis best, 'tis infinitely best,
    To go where tempests never come;
Where saints and angels, ever blest,
    Dwell, and enjoy their heavenly home.

23

Of Being Ever with Christ

Then we which are alive and remain shall be caught up together with them in the clouds, to meet the Lord in the air: and so shall we ever be with the Lord.

1 Thess. iv. 17.

Oh, who can tell what joy shall beam
    On all the ransom'd race,
When they shall join the hallow'd strains
    And see the Saviour's face!

24

Of Reigning with Christ

It is a faithful saying: For if we be dead with him, we shall also live with him: if we suffer, we shall also reign with him. 2 *Tim. ii.* 11, 12.

> Ever upward may we move,
> Wafted on the wings of love:
> Looking when our Lord shall come,
> Longing, gasping after home!
> There may we with thee remain,
> Partners of thine endless reign.

25

Of Being Like Christ

Beloved, now are we the sons of God, and it doth not yet appear what we shall be: but we know that, when he shall appear, we shall be like him; for we shall see him as he is. 1 *John iii.* 2.

> Him eye to eye we there shall see,
>   Our face like his shall shine:
> Oh, what a glorious company,
>   When saints and angels join!

26

Of an Heavenly Habitation

We know that if our earthly house of this tabernacle were dissolved, we have a building of God, an house not made with hands, eternal in the heavens. *2 Cor. v. 1.*

There is a home for weary souls,
    By sin and sorrow driven;
When toss'd on life's tempestuous shoals,
Where storms arise, and ocean rolls,
    'Tis found above—in heaven.

27

Of Perfection of Knowledge in Heaven

Now we see through a glass, darkly; but then face to face: now I know in part; but then shall I know even as also I am known. *1 Cor. xiii. 12.*

As through a glass I dimly see
    The wonders of thy love;
How little do I know of thee,
    Or of the joys above!

'Tis but in part I know thy will—
    I bless thee for the sight—
When will thy love the rest reveal
    In glory's clearer light?

28

Of a Crown of Righteousness

Henceforth there is laid up for me a crown of righteousness, which the Lord, the righteous Judge, shall
give me at that day. *2 Tim. iv. 8.*

> God has laid up in heaven for me
>   A crown which cannot fade;
> The righteous Judge, in that great day,
>   Shall place it on my head.

29

Of Reunion with Glorified Spirits

What is our hope, or joy, or crown of rejoicing? Are
not even ye in the presence of our Lord Jesus Christ at
his coming? *1 Thes. ii. 19.*

> We soon shall join the throng,
>   Their pleasures we shall share,
> And sing the everlasting song
>   With all the ransom'd there:
>   Hallelujah!
>   We are on our way to God.

30

Believer's Anticipations
a Call to Holiness

Wherefore, beloved, seeing that ye look for such things, be diligent that ye may be found of him in peace, without spot, and blameless. *2 Pet. iii. 14.*

Yet with these prospects full in sight
I'll wait thy signal for my flight;
For while thy service I pursue,
I find a heaven in all I do.

DECEMBER

Final Blessedness of the Believer

I

Eternal Life the Gift of God

Now being made free from sin, and become servants to God, ye have your fruit unto holiness, and the end everlasting life. For the wages of sin is death; but the gift of God is eternal life through Jesus Christ our Lord. *Rom. vi. 22, 23.*

From thee, my God, my joys shall rise,
    And run eternal rounds,
Beyond the limits of the skies,
    And all created bounds.

2

Eternal Life the Purchase of Christ

Neither by the blood of goats and calves, but by his own blood he entered in once into the holy place, having obtained eternal redemption for us. *Heb. ix. 12.*

> Pardon and peace to dying men,
>   And endless life are given:
> By the rich blood that Jesus shed
>   Our souls are brought to heaven.

3

Eternal Life Secured by the Spirit

The Holy Spirit of promise is the earnest of our inheritance until the redemption of the purchased possession, unto the praise of his glory. *Eph. i. 13, 14.*

> Dost thou not dwell in all the saints,
>   And seal the heirs of heaven?
> When wilt thou banish my complaints,
>   And show my sins forgiven.

4

Heaven the Desire of the Saints

Whilst we are at home in the body, we are absent from the Lord, we are confident, and willing rather to be absent from the body, and to be present with the Lord.

2 Cor. v. 6, 8.

In that bright city I would dwell,
　With that bless'd church the Saviour
　　praise,
And, safe, redeem'd from death and hell,
　Sit at his feet through endless days.

5

Heaven a Rest

There remaineth a rest to the people of God. *Heb. iv. 9.*

Oh where shall rest be found,
　Rest for the weary soul?
'Twere vain the ocean-depths to sound,
　Or pierce to either pole.

Beyond this vale of tears,
　There is a life above,
Unmeasured by the flight of years—
　And all that life is love.

6

Heaven Compared to a Marriage Supper

Write, Blessed are they which are called unto the marriage supper of the Lamb. *Rev. xix. 9.*

"Worthy the Lamb!" aloud they cry,
    "That brought us here to God:"
In ceaseless hymns of praise they shout
    The merits of his blood.

7

Heaven an Inheritance

He is the mediator of the new testament, that by means of death, for the redemption of the transgressions that were under the first testament, they which are called might receive the promise of eternal inheritance. *Heb. ix. 15.*

There is my house and portion fair,
My treasure and my heart are there,
    And my abiding home;
For me my elder brethren stay,
And angels beckon me away,
    And Jesus bids me come.

8

Heaven a Kingdom

I appoint unto you a kingdom, as my Father hath appointed unto me; that ye may eat and drink at my table in my kingdom. *Luke xxii. 29, 30.*

> O God! O Good beyond compare!
> If all thy meaner works are fair,
> How glorious must that kingdom be,
> Where thy redeem'd shall dwell with thee!

9

Heaven Is Prepared Mansions

In my Father's house are many mansions: if it were not so, I would have told you. I go to prepare a place for you. *John xiv. 2.*

> High in yonder realms of light,
> Far above these lower skies,
> Fair and exquisitely bright,
> Heaven's unfading mansions rise.

> Glad within these bless'd abodes,
> Dwell the' enraptur'd saints above,
> Where no anxious care corrodes,
> Happy in Immanuel's love.

10

Heaven Compared to Paradise

Jesus said unto him, Verily I say unto thee, To-day shalt thou be with me in paradise. *Luke xxiii. 43.*

There is a land of pure delight,
     Where saints immortal reign;
Infinite day excludes the night,
     And pleasures banish pain.

There everlasting spring abides,
     And never-withering flowers:
Death, like a narrow sea, divides
     This heavenly land from ours.

11

Heaven a State of Holiness

There shall in no wise enter into it any thing that defileth, neither whatsoever worketh abomination, or maketh a lie: but they which are written in the Lamb's book of life. *Rev. xxi. 27.*

The soul, from sin for ever free,
     Shall mourn its power no more,
But clothed in spotless purity,
     Redeeming love adore.

12

Heaven a State of Happiness

Thou wilt show me the path of life: in thy presence is
fulness of joy; at thy right hand there are pleasures for
evermore. *Psalm xvi. 11.*

Love, in an ever-deepening tide,
O'er all the plains above
Spreads, like a sea immensely wide—
For God himself is Love.

13

Heaven a State of Service

They serve him day and night in his temple: and he
that sitteth on the throne shall dwell among them.

Rev. vii. 15.

And swift to do his high behest
Each spirit wings its flight;
And virtue glows on every breast,
A gem of purest light.

14

No Sorrow in Heaven

God shall wipe away all tears from their eyes; and there shall be no more death, neither sorrow, nor crying, neither shall there be any more pain: for the former things are passed away. *Rev. xxi. 4.*

Joy and gladness banish sighs,
    Perfect love dispels their fears,
And for ever from their eyes,
    God shall wipe away all tears.

15

No Curse in Heaven

There shall be no more curse: but the throne of God and the Lamb shall be in it. *Rev. xxii. 3.*

When we shall Christ in glory meet,
Our utmost joys shall be complete:
When landed on that heavenly shore,
Death and the curse shall be no more.

16

No Night in Heaven

There shall be no night there; and they need no candle, neither light of the sun; for the Lord God giveth them light: and they shall reign for ever and ever. *Rev. xxii. 5.*

> Nor needed is the shining moon,
>   Nor e'en the sun's bright ray;
> For glory, from the sacred throne,
>   Spreads everlasting day.

17

No Death in Heaven

They which shall be accounted worthy to obtain that world, and the resurrection from the dead, neither marry nor are given in marriage: neither can they die any more: for they are equal unto the angels.

Luke xx. 35, 36.

> There pain and sickness never come,
>   And grief no more complains;
> Health triumphs in immortal bloom,
>   And endless pleasure reigns.

18

Praises of Heaven

They sung a new song, saying, Thou wast slain, and hast redeemed us to God by thy blood out of every kindred, and tongue, and people, and nation. *Rev. v. 9.*

> Hark! hark! the voice of ceaseless praise
>   Around Jehovah's throne,
> Songs of celestial joy they raise,
>   To mortal lips unknown.

19

Society of Heaven

These are they which came out of great tribulation, and have washed their robes, and made them white in the blood of the Lamb: therefore are they before the throne of God. *Rev. vii. 14, 15.*

> Clad in raiment pure and white,
>   Victor-palms in every hand,
> Through their great Redeemer's might,
>   More than conquerors they stand.

20

Saints Shall Be with God

He will dwell with them, and they shall be his people, and God himself shall be with them, and be their God.

Rev. xxi. 3.

Oh glorious hour! oh bless'd abode!
I shall be near and like my God;
And flesh and sin no more control
The sacred pleasures of the soul.

21

Saints Shall Be with Christ

Father, I will that they also, whom thou hast given me, be with me where I am; that they may behold my glory. *John xvii. 24.*

Oh then shall the veil be remov'd,
    And round me thy brightness be pour'd:
I shall meet Him whom absent I lov'd,
    I shall see Him whom unseen I ador'd!

22

Saints Shall Inherit All Things

He that overcometh shall inherit all things; and I will be his God, and he shall be my son. *Rev. xxi. 7.*

> The saints in his presence receive
>> Their great and eternal reward;
> With Jesus in heaven they live;
>> They reign in the smile of their Lord.

23

Saints Shall Be Perfect

Ye are come unto the general assembly and church of the first-born, which are written in heaven, and to God the Judge of all, and to the spirits of just men made perfect. *Heb. xii. 22, 23.*

> A life in heaven! oh what is this?
>> The sum of all that faith believed;
> Fullness of joy, and perfect bliss,
>> Unseen—unfathom'd—unconceiv'd.

24

Saints Shall Be Glorious in Appearance

Then shall the righteous shine forth as the sun in the kingdom of their Father. *Matt. xiii. 43.*

The Lamb is their light and their sun,
    And, lo, by reflection they shine;
With Jesus ineffably one,
    And bright in effulgence divine.

25

Saints Shall Be Honoured as Victors

I beheld, and, lo, a great multitude, which no man could number, of all nations, and kindreds, and people, and tongues, stood before the throne, and before the Lamb, clothed with white robes, and palms in their hands. *Rev. vii. 9.*

Now the conquerors bring their palms
    To the Lamb amidst the throne,
And proclaim in joyful psalms,
    Victory through his cross alone.

26

Saints Shall Be Kings
and Priests unto God

Thou hast made us unto our God kings and priests:
and we shall reign on the earth. *Rev. v. 10.*

Thou hast redeem'd our souls with blood,
  Hast set the prisoners free,
Hast made us kings and priests to God,
  And we shall reign with thee.

27

Joys of Heaven Are Sure

Oh how great is thy goodness, which thou hast laid up
for them that fear thee; which thou hast wrought for
them that trust in thee before the sons of men!

Psalm xxxi. 19.

This is the hope that shall sustain me
  Till life's pilgrimage be past;
Fears may vex, and troubles pain me,
  I shall reach my home at last.

28

Joys of Heaven Are Abundant

The Lamb which is in the midst of the throne shall feed them, and shall lead them unto living fountains of water. *Rev. vii.* 17.

The Lamb that fills the middle throne
  Shall shed around his milder beams,
There shall they feast on his rich love,
  And drink full joys from heavenly streams.

29

Joys of Heaven Are Satisfying

I will behold thy face in righteousness: I shall be satisfied, when I awake, with thy likeness. *Psalm xvii.* 15.

Oh! when awaken'd by thy care,
Thy face I view, thy image bear,
How shall my breast with transport glow!
What full delight my heart o'erflow!

30

Joys of Heaven Are Eternal

Him that overcometh will I make a pillar in the temple of my God, and he shall go no more out. *Rev. iii. 12.*

The everlasting doors
    Shall soon the saints receive,
Above, with angel powers,
    In glorious joy to live:
Far from a world of grief and sin,
With God eternally shut in.

31

Believers to Wait for Heaven

Blessed is he that waiteth, and cometh to the thousand three hundred and five and thirty days. But go thou thy way till the end be: for thou shalt rest, and stand in thy lot at the end of the days. *Dan. xii, 12, 13.*

Jerusalem, my happy home,
    My soul still pants for thee;
When shall my labours have an end
    In joy, and peace, and thee.

A Note on the Type

The text of this book was set in a digitalized version of Garamond No. 3, a modern rendering of the type first cut by Claude Garamond (c. 1480–1561). Garamond was a pupil of Geoffroy Tory and is believed to have based his letters on the Venetian models, although he introduced a number of important differences, and it is to him we owe the letter which we know as "old style." He gave to his letters a certain elegance and a feeling of movement that won for their creator an immediate reputation and the patronage of Francis I of France.